Thomas M. Stubbs,
Dillard, Ga.,
Sept., 1963.

The Five Royal Governors
of North Carolina 1729-1775

D1607484

The Five Royal Governors
of North Carolina
1729-1775

By
Blackwell P. Robinson, Ph. D.

Professor of History
Woman's College of the University of North Carolina

A Publication of
The Carolina Charter Tercentenary Commission
Box 1881, Raleigh, North Carolina

1963

Rare
F
257
.R6

THE CAROLINA CHARTER TERCENTENARY COMMISSION

Hon. Francis E. Winslow, *Chairman*

Henry Belk
Mrs. Doris Betts
Dr. Chalmers G. Davidson
Mrs. Everett L. Durham
William C. Fields
William Carrington Gretter, Jr.
Grayson Harding
Mrs. James M. Harper, Jr.
Mrs. Ernest L. Ives
Dr. Henry W. Jordan

Mrs. Kauno A. Lehto
James G. W. MacLamroc
Mrs. Harry McMullan
Dr. Paul Murray
Dan M. Paul
Dr. Robert H. Spiro, Jr.
David Stick
J. P. Strother
Mrs. J. O. Tally, Jr.
Rt. Rev. Thomas H. Wright

Ex-Officio

Dr. Charles F. Carroll,
Superintendent of
Public Instruction

Robert L. Stallings,
Director, Department of
Conservation and Development

Dr. Christopher Crittenden
Director, Department of
Archives and History,
Secretary

The Carolina Charter Tercentenary Commission was established by the North Carolina General Assembly to "make plans and develop a program for celebration of the tercentenary of the granting of the Carolina Charter of 1663 . . ." As part of this program the Commission arranged for the publication of a number of historical pamphlets for use in stimulating interest in the study of North Carolina history during the period 1663-1763. This publication is part of that project.

Raleigh, North Carolina, 1963

CONTENTS

INTRODUCTION

Charles I, King of Great Britain and Ireland, was beheaded in 1649 by Oliver Cromwell and his Model Army of Puritans. But the rule of Oliver and his weaker son, Richard, became increasingly unpopular. In a very real sense the English people had exchanged a lawful although tyrannical monarch for an upstart, puritanical despot. And so, in 1660, Charles II, the "Merrie Monarch," was restored to the throne of his father. Having no desire to "go on his travels again"—as he expressed it—he made a very statesman-like decision: He would make a tremendous grant of land in the New World to eight of the wealthiest and most influential men in England—all supporters of his and of his father. This would have the double-barreled effect of expressing his appreciation to these loyal friends and, more important, would ensure their continued support to his still somewhat shaky throne. The Carolina Charter of 1663 was the result. By this great document eight Lords Proprietors were granted all territory in North America between 36 and 31 degrees north latitude and extending westward to the South Seas. This comprised an area bounded today by a line running a little south of present Edenton, Durham, and Greensboro (North Carolina) on the north, to approximately the present Georgia-Florida border, and westward to the Pacific Ocean, which they referred to as the South Seas. Two years later this grant was extended 30 minutes to the north (approximately the present North Carolina-Virginia border), to include the already settled Albemarle section of northeastern North Carolina, and two degrees to the south (approximately the location of St. Augustine, Florida) to represent a direct thrust at the Spanish fort there.

As the decades rolled by, however, there was an ever-increasing demand for the centralization of all His Majesty's colonies by royalizing them, or bringing them under direct royal authority and control. The Lords Proprietors of Carolina at first quite naturally resisted all efforts to take over their twin colonies* until they finally realized it was a losing battle. Rather than lose them without any repayment or reimbursement, seven of the proprietors agreed to sell their shares to the Crown for a lump sum of £17,500 (approximately $87,500) or £2,500 (approximately $12,500) each. The eighth share was owned by Lord Carteret, who refused to sell. His interests were consolidated into a region comprising roughly the upper half of North Carolina which later became known as the Granville District. This arrangement would later cause many headaches, not only for the royal governors of the colony, but also for the state.

Thus, in 1729, North and South Carolina became royal colonies under the direct authority (with the exception of the Granville District) of George II.

According to Professor Hugh T. Lefler of the University of North Carolina, this transfer to the Crown marked no significant change in the structure of government, on either the provincial or local level. More specifically:

. . . The powers and duties of governor, council, assembly, courts and local officers were unchanged, though the Crown, instead of the Proprietors, now commissioned and instructed the governor. As a royal colony, North Carolina became more closely identified with the imperial system and had a much closer relationship to the King and Privy Council and to various British administrative agencies, notably the Board of Trade, the Secretary of State for the Southern Department, the Treasury Board, War Board, Admiralty Board, and the Commissioners of the Customs. †

---

*After 1712 a distinction was made between North and South Carolina.
† Hugh T. Lefler and Albert R. Newsome, *North Carolina: The History of A Southern State* (Chapel Hill: The University of North Carolina Press, 1954), p. 138.

In an over-all effort to bring about uniformity among the colonies and to exercise greater control over them, George II and his ministers adopted certain general policies, though they were not strictly enforced. Their chief objective was to set up a far-flung British empire which would be self-sufficient and which would rival or—better— outstrip the French, Spanish, Portuguese, and Dutch empires. To achieve this, a closer control over the American colonies and a closer connection among the colonies were necessary. Practically speaking, this meant that the royal officials—notably the governor, his councillors, and the judges—must be servants of the Crown and be as independent as possible of the colonial assemblies which were elected by the people of the colonies who were qualified to vote. As a result, there developed a tug-of-war between the "governor's party," on the one side, and the "popular party" or the "people's party," on the other. This struggle was further complicatd by the fact that the Crown, rather than paying the salaries of the governor and other provincial officials, made them dependent on the colonial assemblies.

It was against this background that the five royal governors —torn between a loyalty to the Crown and a financial dependence on the assemblies—had to operate. Suffice it to say that few administrators in world history have operated under more trying circumstances.

In order to avoid any confusion, it should be pointed out that, in the absence of a royal governor (because of the delays in appointments and arrivals from across the Atlantic), the president of the governor's council served as acting governor. There were, therefore, five royal governors (*italics*) and four acting governors:

1729-1731	Richard Everard	Held office until Burrington arrived
1731-1734	*George Burrington*	
1734-1752	*Gabriel Johnston*	
1752-1753	Nathaniel Rice	President of the Council
1753-1754	Matthew Rowan	President of the Council
1754-1765	*Arthur Dobbs*	
1765-1771	*William Tryon*	
1771	James Hasell	President of the Council
1771-1775	*Josiah Martin*	

CHAPTER I

George Burrington
1724-1725–1731-1734

George Burrington has the distinction of having been governor of the province of North Carolina twice. He received his first appointment from the Lords Proprietors and his second from the English King.

Governor Charles Eden, after having held office for eight years, died on March 26, 1722, but it was not until February 26, 1723, that King George I, at a session of the Royal Council, gave his approval to the appointment by the Lords Proprietors of Burrington as governor of North Carolina.

Burrington's family had lived for a long time in the county of Devon, where it is assumed he was born. Incidentally, it was this same county which had produced other men who were closely associated with North Carolina, though before it was so named: Sir Walter Raleigh, Sir Francis Drake, and Sir Richard Grenville, each of whom had played a significant role in the early history of Roanoke Island. At any rate, perhaps some of their spirit of adventure was breathed down a century and a half to George Burrington who would seek his fame and fortune in North Carolina.

It is claimed that his family acquired royal favor from the fact that one of its members was the first person of the rank of gentleman who joined William of Orange (who ruled jointly with his wife, as William and Mary) when he first set foot on English soil in 1688.

Neither the exact place of Burrington's birth nor the year of his birth is known, though it was approximately 1680. Nor is there any record of his early years or education.

He actually first entered recorded history when, because of his family's favor in the eyes of the House of Hanover, he was granted a captain's commission in the British army. Later, in 1732, he was able to proclaim proudly:

> I have served the crown in every reign since the Abdication of King James, always was allowed to behave as became a Man of Honour, and the Family whose name I bear; their Services at the Revolution [the Glorious Revolution of 1688 when William and Mary mounted the English throne] and during the life of King William of glorious memory I hope are not yet in Oblivion.

Some months after his appointment as governor of North Carolina, Burrington set out for his new seat of government. He landed at Edenton, the colonial capital, where he took

BURRINGTON COAT-OF-ARMS

From Marshall DeLancey Haywood, *Governor George Burrington, With an Account of His Official Administrations in the Colony of North Carolina, 1724-1725, 1731-1734.* Raleigh: Edwards & Broughton, 1896.

Copy in the North Carolina Collection, University of North Carolina Library, Chapel Hill.

the oath of office on January 15, 1724. Though he held the imposing title of "Governor General and Admiral of the Province," he was not given a very flattering reception. Within the year his person was insulted and his authority defied.

The chief trouble in the beginning lay in the fact that, after the death of Governor Eden and until Burrington's arrival, affairs of state had been administered by Colonel William Reed, as President of the Council. Reed's brief taste of power had gone to his head and he deeply resented having to yield to another man. He therefore set out deliberately to undermine Burrington's authority and reputation. He first circulated the story that Burrington had been imprisoned in England for beating an old woman, though there is no evidence as to its verity.

On another occasion the governor sent a direct order to Reed as President of the Council. When the messenger tried to deliver the written order to Reed he refused to accept it, saying, "I do not value the Governor's orders." Whereupon the messenger laid it on the table, saying, "I will leave it here, Mr. Reed, as I was ordered to do." Reed's reply was heated: "I am not Mr. Reed, sir! I would have you know, sir, I am President Reed."

Such incidents and rumors as these—arising from a man of Reed's prestige—quite naturally tended to undermine Burrington's authority in the eyes of the colonists and to lead others to make derogatory remarks against the governor. Perhaps the worst verbal attack against Burrington was one by Joseph Castleton, of Albemarle County, while he was in England:

The Governor is a damn rogue and villain. There ain't a worse rogue and villain in the world. A fellow came to him once for justice and what do you think he got? The old rogue beat him, made him kneel down to him and beg for his life. When I go back home I'm going to write to all the Lords Proprietors and tell them what a rogue the Governor is.

It might be added when Castleton returned to the province, he was indicted by the General Court (which is comparable to the present State Supreme Court) for attempting to stir up sedition and tumult and bring the governor into disrepute. He pleaded guilty and humbly requested the mercy of the court. He was sentenced to stand in the pillory on the public parade ground in Edenton from twelve until two in the afternoon and, in addition, to beg on his knees for pardon from the governor.

Burrington's first administration was destined to be short-lived. The man who played the key role in bringing it to an abrupt end was the highly respected Chief Justice of North Carolina, Christopher Gale. It appears—or so Gale charged—that shortly after the governor's arrival he gave out repeated threats against the Chief Justice, saying he would slit his nose, crop his ears, and lay him in irons. Gale also alleged that Burrington had insulted him in open court and had attempted to enter his house,

> but finding he could not break open the door, he broke the window all to pieces, cursing and threatning him in a grievous manner, swearing a great many oaths, that he would lay him by the heels, nay would have him by the throat, speedily, and burn his house or blow it up with gun-powder.

So serious did Gale feel about the governor's attacks upon him that he set sail for England to prefer charges—backed by seven members of the Provincial Council—before the Lords Proprietors. Such an indictment by such a powerful and respected man quite understandably led the Lords to remove Burrington from office. He was succeeded by Sir Richard Everard, an English baronet, who took office July 17, 1725.

In the light of the accusations against Burrington and the action of the Lords Proprietors, it is interesting to note that the next assembly forwarded to the Proprietors an address in which they expressed the "great happiness which the Province lately enjoy'd" under Burrington and their displeasure at the "Sudden & Unexpected Change which had been made thro' the many false & malicious Calumnies raised against that gentleman by Persons of the most Vile Characters as well as Desperate fortunes." It also referred to Burrington's "Carryage & behaviour being very Affable & courteous, his Justice very Exemplary, & his care and Industry to promote the Interest & welfare of the Province very Eminent & Conspicuous."

Burrington's attacks on the new governor were as vicious as they had been against Gale. He presented himself before Everard's house and called out in a blustery voice: "I want satisfaction of you, therefore come out and give it to me." When Sir Richard refused, he

> proceeded to vent wrath in a diversified and well-chosen collection of profanity, among other things characterizing him as a calf's head, noodle, and an ape, who was no more fit to be Governor than Sancho Panza.

This incident was followed by abusive attacks upon two other colonists in their homes. As a result, Burrington was indicted by the attorney general, but he failed to appear for trial. After being continued for several terms, the cases were finally disposed of by the legal means of a *nol pros* (short for "I do not wish to prosecute" in Latin). Shortly afterwards, Burrington left Edenton, but, as has been mentioned, he would return in 1731.

In 1729 seven of the Lords Proprietors with the exception of Lord Granville, as we have seen, surrendered their rights to the Crown and North Carolina became a royal colony. With this change of affairs, Burrington set out to win friends and influence important people in London in order to regain his lost governorship. Despite the efforts of Gale and others to prevent the re-appointment, Burrington, largely through the influence of the Duke of Newcastle, received his commission as the first Royal Governor of North Carolina on January 15, 1730. It would be over a year, though, before he arrived in Edenton and took the oath of office—February 25, 1731.

Oddly enough his re-appointment was generally hailed with approval throughout the province. The Grand Jury of the province and the assembly both sent addresses of thanks to His Royal Majesty, thanking him for his thoughtfulness in the appointment of Burrington,

> who by his Behaviour during the time he governed this Province . . . rendred himself very agreeable to the People by the Great Care he then shewed in his due Administration of Justice and in promoting the welfare of the Province."

Burrington replied to these flattering remarks by saying that he was at a loss for words to express the esteem and regard he had for persons of such great worth and excellent qualifications. It looked, therefore, as if all would be sweetness and light, but the honeymoon was soon over. His first assembly, which met April 13,1731, requested Burrington to issue a proclamation to suppress the charging of exorbitant fees by public officials. Rather than agreeing, he sent the members of the assembly an insulting refusal and shortly prorogued them (sent them home) because of their "divisions, heats, and indecencies."

Regardless, though, of his faults, whims, and eccentricities, Burrington was zealous in his efforts to improve the province. Indeed, he worked and traveled untiringly for its betterment —at a time when travel was both fatiguing and hazardous. On one occasion he wrote Lord Carteret that several times he narrowly escaped starvation and that he had come near drowning more than once. He also made it a habit to visit every new settlement in the province and to inspect roads and bridges to see that they were being properly maintained.

It was Burrington, moreover, who was chiefly responsible for the development of the Cape Fear region around the ports of Brunswick and Wilmington. Here he purchased a tract of some ten thousand acres and offered inducements for people to settle it. It was Burrington, too, who succeeded in pushing to completion a highway from New Bern to the settlements farther south, and another, longer one was undertaken at his instance from the Virginia border to the banks of the Cape Fear. It was also he who discovered and marked the channel of that river and of Topsail Inlet. He also explored other waterways which had been relatively unknown.

In return for his great labors in the field of internal improvements the assembly saw fit to extend to him a vote of thanks. Even more complimentary was "The Honble. Address of the Inhabitants of Bertie & Edgecombe precincts," delivered in October, 1735, to Burrington's successor, Gabriel Johnston. It stated, in part, that

> . . . no man living could have taken more pains & fatigue than Burrington did to acquaint himself with this Province in General which his many Journeys & travels into the backwoods on foot will Justifie, Sometimes, accompanied by one man Only & often pinched with hunger (nay) in danger of Perishing having but one biscutie for three days to subsist on and sometimes Coming amongst the Inhabitts without a Ragg of Cloaths

to his back perhaps 200 miles from the place he set out
Often carrying with him Considerable Sums of money &
disposeing of it amongst many poor people . . .

Though most of the people genuinely appreciated Burrington's great efforts to improve conditions in the colony,
his intolerant disposition and his abusive conduct, if he
were opposed, made for him many enemies, some of whom
were among the most influential in the province. This was
especially true of the Attorney General of the colony, John
Montgomery, and three members of the Governor's Council—
Nathaniel Rice, John Baptista Ashe, and Edmund Porter.
Ashe and Burrington had a dispute over the ownership of
two horses, as a result of which Ashe was imprisoned for
libel, although he later was released by the Chief Justice.

Montgomery received worse treatment. During a dispute,
the governor in a fit of anger threw Montgomery to the
floor and proceeded to punch him with his knee so that he
might have been killed if bystanders had not rescued him.
Montgomery thereafter asked for permission to return to
England, but Burrington delayed action on the request until
the Council could meet, after which he said he would give
Montgomery permission to go to the Devil. The governor
also challenged him to a duel, but Montgomery did not take
it up. In later life Burrington charged Montgomery of having conspired with Chief Justice Smith and Nathaniel Rice,
the Secretary of the colony, to murder the governor with
pistols. Burrington claimed his life was saved only by the in-
tervention of friends. He asserted that he had all three
indicted for murder, but that they fled to Virginia where
they remained until Governor Gabriel Johnston arrived and
dropped the prosecution.

Under such conditions it is small wonder that Burrington
requested to be relieved of his office. In fact, as Colonel

William L. Saunders wrote, it is amazing that Burrington escaped with his neck: "If a tithe of what his enemies said about Burrington be true, the wonder is that he got away from the colony alive, and not that an attempt was made to kill him."

The Lords of Trade in England (which had charge of colonial affairs) were no doubt saved from an embarrassing situation by his request for recall. Surely Burrington's despatches, which were intemperate and highly colored, must have conveyed to them the impression that he was unfit for the job. At any rate, Gabriel Johnston was commissioned governor in the spring of 1733 and arrived in November, 1734, to relieve Burrington, who was straining at the bit to get away to England.

Other factors contributing to Burrington's desire to leave were expressed in a letter to his friend, the Duke of Newcastle:

> Haveing lived in this Province some years without receiving any money from the King, or Country, was constrained to sell not only my household goods, but even linnen, plate, and Books, and mortgage my lands and stocks. The many sicknesses that seized me, and their long continuance, have greatly impaired my constitution and substance. My affairs and health being in a bad condition, I humbly desire my Lord Duke will be pleased to obtain His Majesties leave for my return to England.

Something of his impatience may also be seen when he wrote:

> I daily expect the Kings leave for my return to England; when it arrives, shall make haste to London. Hope to inform my Lords of Trade of all that is necessary for his Majesties Service in N. Carolina.

So it must have been with a feeling of relief when, on November 13, 1734, he was present in the General Assembly

SEASONABLE

CONSIDERATIONS

On the Expediency of a

WAR with *France*;

Arising from a faithful Review of the State
of both Kingdoms.

To which are added

A POSTSCRIPT, on the List of
the *French* Army,

A short COMPARISON, between the *British*
and *French* Dominions;

And a STATE of the *French* Revenues, and
Forces in the Year, 1701.

By *GEORGE BURRINGTON*, Esq;

LONDON:

Printed for F. COGAN, at the *Middle Temple-gate.*

MDCCXLIII:

(Price One Shilling.)

TITLEPAGE OF PAMPHLET BY GEORGE BURRINGTON

From copy in the North Carolina Collection, University of North
Carolina Library, Chapel Hill.

when the proclamation announcing Johnston's arrival was read.

After his return to England, little is known of his career, which ended mysteriously in February, 1759, except that he was the author of at least two books: *Seasonable Considerations on the Expediency of a War with France*, which was published in 1743, and *An Answer to Dr. William Brakenridge's Letter Concerning the Number of Inhabitants within the London Bills of Mortality*.

As to his death, we only know that he was murdered, perhaps a case of robbery, in the Bird Cage Walk in St. James' Park in London and that his body was later found in the nearby canal.

In any appraisal of his life, perhaps the conclusions of Colonel Saunders are the most valid:

> . . . he stands out . . . as a man of ability, but utterly disqualified by grievous faults for the position he occupied. And yet he was a wiser ruler than his predecessor, Everard, and possessed no more faults; he was, too, to say the least, as wise as his successor, Gabriel Johnston, and no more arbitrary. Certain it is, too, that the province under the administration continued to flourish and greatly prosper, both in wealth and population. It may be that Burrington was hampered by his instructions from the Crown, and that no Governor could have carried them out and kept the peace with a people who, as he said, were subtle and crafty to admiration, who could neither be outwitted nor cajoled, who always behaved insolently to their Governors, who maintained that their money could not be taken from them save by appropriations made by their own House of Assembly . . .

CHAPTER II

Gabriel Johnston
1734-1752

Gabriel Johnston sat in the governor's chair of North Carolina longer than any other governor, royal, proprietary, or state. In fact for eighteen years, from 1734 to 1752, he managed to serve his Royal Master, George II, and the people of the province. This in itself was no mean feat, equalled or exceeded by few royal governors in English America, though Sir William Berkeley presided over the colony of Virginia for a third of a century, from 1642 to 1677.

Born in 1699 in the Lowlands of Scotland at a place called Annandale, this intrepid Scot left little recorded history of his early life. It is known that he attended St. Andrews University, located near Dundee on a bay of the North Sea. St. Andrews, incidentally, is the generally recognized birthplace of golf clubs and associations, though there is no evidence that Johnston ever participated in this "royal and ancient" sport. It is known, however, that he studied for the medical profession, though he does not seem to have entered it. Instead, he studied languages and became a professor of Oriental languages at his *alma mater*. Apparently attracted by politics or by the lure of the city, he moved to London. Here he was engaged in political writing with Lord Bolingbroke and Spencer Compton, the Earl of Wilmington. The latter was a Lord of the Treasury and an opponent of Sir Robert Walpole, the first Prime Minister of Great Britain.

It was probably this Earl of Wilmington who was responsible for Johnston's appointment as governor of North Carolina in 1734. The fact that Johnston renamed the Cape Fear settlement of New Town (later Newton) for Wilmington points to this conclusion. At any rate, Johnston landed at the old port of Brunswick, thirty miles below Wilmington, and took the oath of his new office November 2, 1734. And so he began a long reign which would continue until his death.

The new governor, sent to take the place of Governor George Burrington, who had returned to England, had not amassed enough wealth to pay his passage across the Atlantic and buy property in his new seat of government. But he was able to secure the necessary advance funds from an Ulster Scot, Henry McCulloh, who had become a London merchant and one of the largest land speculators in America. In return for promising to import 6,000 Protestant settlers, McCulloh had acquired some 1,200,000 acres of land, principally along the Cape Fear River. No doubt he willingly advanced Johnston the necessary funds in the hope of securing the governor's assistance in his plans. As matters turned out, however, he and Johnston reached the parting of the ways, and McCulloh did not hesitate to accuse him of neglect and maladministration, or poor management of the governor's office.

Johnston had hardly arrived when he ran into trouble with the powerful Moore family of Brunswick, headed by "King" Roger Moore of Orton plantation (still in operation) and Colonel Maurice Moore, who had given the 320 acres on which the port town of Brunswick was located. Determined to establish a new port of entry at Wilmington, some thirty miles higher up the Cape Fear River and thus farther removed from hostile attack by the Spanish and French, Johnston so maneuvered and manipulated the colonial assembly that he succeeded in his objective.

At Wilmington, Johnston then set up a Court of Exchequer

(a sort of tax court) to decide all questions regarding quit-rents. These were a relic of the old feudal system in England which were so-called because they acquitted or freed the tenant of all dues and services to the feudal lord for a small money payment. In America they were small annual payments of money to the colonial governor as agent of the Crown.

In addition to the Court of Exchequer, Johnston established a court at Wilmington with the rather curious title of the Court of Oyer and Terminer. This meant that all legal business would be carried on in Wilmington, thereby lessening further the importance of Brunswick. The final blow to the latter town was delivered when the governor appointed one James Murray as naval officer at Wilmington to handle port and customs matters.

But while Johnston might have won his point in regard to developing a new port at Wilmington, the quitrent problem was not so easily solved. To begin with, it was extremely unpopular for a number of reasons. It was not based on the value of the land or the ability of the taxpayer to pay. Moreover, the rate had been doubled when the King took over direct control of the colony in 1729, so that the usual rate was now four shillings (about eighty cents) for every one hundred acres of land (this was twice as high as it was in the Granville Grant or in the sister colony of Virginia). To add further insult to injury, the King put in the exasperating provision that quitrents must be paid in specie (hard money, coins, gold and silver), which was extremely scarce in the colony, and that it was the duty of the taxpayer to bring his payment to certain designated places, rather than having the collectors come to his plantation or farm to collect. This was a very real hardship, because of the woeful condition of transportation.

The resolute Scottish governor was determined to carry out the instructions of his Royal Master to the last degree, despite the angered resistance of the people who justly felt imposed upon. The latter argued that the entire colony did not contain the necessary amount of "hard" money and that they had always paid quitrents in "kind," that is, with produce grown on their farms, and that they had always made payment to a tax-collector on their own farms. They based their rights on the Carolina Charter of 1663 and were determined to stand by them.

Supporting the small farmers in their stand against Johnston and the English government were such great landowners as Edward Moseley (a former Speaker of the House), the powerful Moore family, and ex-Governor Burrington. Moreover, a group of landholders in Bertie and Edgecombe counties drew up a petition, demanding a return to the old form of collection. When Johnston turned a deaf ear to the complaints, a mob marched on Edenton in an attempt to free a prisoner who it was thought had been imprisoned for refusing to pay his taxes. Although the mob broke up before it reached Edenton, the unrest and dissatisfaction would continue down to the Revolution.

Johnston, meanwhile, was in a bad situation. How could he please both the King and the settlers? He wrote letters to the all-important Board of Trade which handled colonial matters in the King's name. But that body—busy with other affairs of government—failed to answer.

Realizing that the distressing situation would have to be solved in some way, Johnston managed to get a new quitrents bill—a compromise—through the assembly in 1739. This bill, he hoped, would satisfy both sides, but when it reached England it was "disallowed," or vetoed, by the King on the advice of his ministers, probably because it permitted payments in commodities. As a result, the struggle over quit-rents and their payment continued to plague successive royal governors without letup.

Many other problems—some large, some small—gave Johnston grave concern. One of these, which seems strange to us today, was the problem of the destruction of crops by birds and beasts of the forest. Reports handed down to us reveal that birds and fowl destroyed peas, wheat, and Indian-corn; that parakeets ruined entire crops of apples; that foxes, raccoons, hawks, etc., devoured many chickens; that bears devoured swine; and that every wolf did £20 to £30 damage to crops yearly. The situation became so alarming that Johnston, in 1736, devoted a large portion of his annual message to his assembly to the problem. He recommended offering rewards for killing such above mentioned "vermin" in the following words:

> For the better preserving your Cattle, Corn, and other grains, I believe you will find it highly necessary to provide a sufficient reward for the Killing of Vermin which I am informed have done great Mischief in most parts of the Province.

As a consequence, the assembly passed a law which offered rewards for the killing of such destructive vermin.

Another concern to worry the governor was the distressing condition of religion. Although the Church of England (or the Anglican Church, or the Established Church) had been instituted in Carolina by English law, it was never very strong or popular during these early times. But every royal governor received instructions from England to see that laws were passed for its support. Burrington had failed to get any such laws passed, though he had tried hard. The situation was made more difficult by the rise of other denominations of "dissenters," especially the Quakers, who were strong in the Albemarle section.

Johnston, with his customary vigor, attempted to carry out his instructions. After some investigation he reported to the assembly of 1739 that the state of religion in the colony was "really scandalous" and that there was a "deplorable and almost total want of divine worship throughout the province." Only at Bath, the first incorporated town in North Carolina (1705), and Edenton, the political center, were church services held regularly. He therefore implored the assembly to remedy the situation "without loss of time."

As a result of Johnston's insistence, the assembly passed the Vestry Act of 1741, but again the King, on the recommendation of his Privy Council (or private cabinet) disallowed it because it gave to the individual vestries (or local church governing bodies) the sole right of selecting their rectors, or ministers. This right, it was thought, belonged only to the King and the Anylican bishops. Later Vestry Acts met with the same fate, until Governor Arthur Dobbs in 1765 was able to secure one which was acceptable to the Privy Council, mainly because there was no reference to the method of selecting the vestry.

Equally distressing to the Scotsman, who had great respect for education, was the lack of schools and learning in the colony. In 1736 he addressed the assembly in the typical language and spelling of that day:

> In all civilized Societys of men, it has always been looked upon as a matter of the greatest consequence to their Peace and happiness, to polish the minds of young Persons with some degree of learning, and early to instill into them the Principles of virtue and religion, and that the Legislature has never yet taken the least care to erect one school, which deserves the name in this wide extend-

ed country, must in the judgement of all thinking men, be reckoned one of our greatest misfortunes.

The assembly replied by agreeing heartily, but took no steps to correct the situation:

> We lament very much the want of Divine Publick Worship (a crying scandal in any, but more especially in a Church Community;) as well as the general neglect in point of education, the main sources of all Disorders and Corruptions, which we should rejoice to see removed and remedyed, and are ready to do our parts, towards the reformation of such flagrant and prolifick Evils.

However, Johnston was more successful in another field. For a long time there had been a crying need to have the laws of the colony revised and printed, but there was no printer in the entire colony. Johnston was deeply concerned over the situation and in 1736, 1739, 1740, and 1744 urged the assembly to do something about this "shameful condition." Finally, in 1746, the assembly appointed four commissioners to revise and print the laws of the colony. In 1749 the revisal, written almost entirely by Samuel Swann, was presented to the assembly. Meanwhile it appointed James Davis as the colony's first public printer to print the revisal and other official documents. Davis accordingly set up the first printing press in North Carolina at New Bern in 1749 and later, incidentally, printed the first newspaper in the colony, *The North Carolina Gazette*. In 1751, he published what is considered the first book published in North Carolina. It is usually referred to as "The Yellow Jacket," because of the color of its binding, or as "Swann's Revisal," but its official title is *A Collection of all the Public Acts of Assembly, of the Province of North Carolina: Now in Force and Use.*

And so, a year before Johnston's death, his efforts in this regard were rewarded. Certainly Johnston should be given due credit for his part in urging this important project.

The most ever-present problem of his entire administration—and that of the other royal governors—was the problem of his salary. As has been noted already, the governor was a royal agent, a servant of the King and his lieutenant in the colony. As such he was not really responsible to the assembly or to the people. And yet he was dependent upon the colonial assembly for his salary. It is easy to see what an effective weapon this could be: either the governor signed the assembly's bills into law, however much they displeased him, or they withheld his salary.

Though Johnston boasted of his "management" of the assembly, the facts do not bear out the claim. Four years after he came over he wrote to England that he had received only £200 ($1,000) of salary, which, he said, was not enough "for living with common decency." Again, in 1746, he wrote the Board of Trade that he had received no salary for eight years.

Something of his unhappy plight may be seen in a letter he wrote the Board of Trade about trying to meet with his council:

> It is with great difficulty we make shift to meet twice a year. All the rest of our time is spent at our own little plantations which are some fifty, some a hundred, and some two hundred miles distant from one another, and this will always be our case until our salaries are regularly paid . . . which makes it impossible for us to remain long in any of the towns of this province where, small and despicable as they are, living is dearer than in London.

Johnston's hopes for a regularly paid salary were never realized and at the time of his death in 1752 his salary was in arrears for fourteen years.

Incidentally, legal battles over his estate lasted until 1798. His nephew, Samuel Johnston, who would become the sixth governor of the State of North Carolina, received a substantial part of the final division.

Another dispute which Johnston inherited from his predecessor, Burrington, involved the dividing line between North and South Carolina. Burrington and Governor Robert Johnson of South Carolina had agreed before the Board of Trade in London in 1730 that the line should begin thirty miles southwest of the Cape Fear and run that distance parallel to the river throughout its entire course. Back in North Carolina, however, Burrington refused to go through with the agreement and thus matters hung when Johnston took office.

Again he acted with swiftness. In 1735 he and Governor Johnson of South Carolina appointed commissioners to make a survey of the line. It is believed that Gabriel Johnston himself used his influence over the conference, which lasted for six weeks, to reach an agreement between the commissioners of the two colonies. At any rate, they agreed that the line should begin thirty miles below the mouth of the Cape Fear River and run in a northwest direction up to the thirty-fifth parallel "and from thence due west to the South Seas." But at no point should it be nearer than thirty miles from the river. Also, if they ran into the lands belonging to the Cherokee or Catawba Indians, they should go around them to the north, thus leaving them in South Carolina.

That same year of 1735—from May until November—the commissioners performed the difficult task of running the line "thro' Desert and uninhabited Woods in many places absolutely impossible." By November they had reached the Little Pee Dee River, some hundred miles from the Atlantic. Two years later they extended it twenty-two more miles to a point they supposed to be on the thirty-fifth parallel.

Johnston insisted later that it shoud be carried farther west, but no further surveys were made until 1765.

Again, however, Gabriel Johnston had used his influence to achieve a worthy goal.

Johnston also fell heir to a sectional conflict between two geographical sections of the colony. To the north there was the older and more populous Albemarle section, which was composed of the precincts—later counties—of Chowan, Currituck, Pasquotank, Perquimans and Tyrrell, all of which had five seats each in the assembly. Included in this group was Bertie precinct with three representatives and Northampton with two. Opposed to these were ten precincts in the Bath area with two seats apiece, while the borough towns (which had the right to send their own delegate) of Wilmington, Edenton, Bath, and New Bern had one each. Therefore it will be seen that Albemarle had thirty-one seats out of a total of fifty-four.

Such a situation was naturally displeasing to the settlers of the southern region and especially to Johnston, whose chief interests and landholdings lay in the Cape Fear region. The assembly, moreover, had been meeting in Edenton, thus making it the unofficial capital of the province. But Johnston wanted to establish a permanent capital in the southern area. He therefore called the assembly to meet in Wilmington in the winter of 1741, hoping that the distant Albemarle members would not be able to come and that he could induce the southern members to establish a permanent southern capital. Much to his dismay, the Albemarle delegates showed up and thereby blocked his plan. Finally, after numerous defeats at the hands of the Albemarle delegates in the next five years, Johnston's achieved his objectives when the assembly passed a law fixing the permanent seat of government at New Bern and reducing the number of delegates of the Albemarle counties to two each. These important acts were passed by only fifteen out of fifty-four delegates present and with all the Albemarle members absent.

Quite naturally the Albemarle counties protested to Johnston and to the Board of Trade against the trickery of what they called this "rump assembly." In the next election—in February, 1747—they ignored the new law and elected their usual five delegates each. As might be expected, the assembly refused to seat them and called for a new election of two each from each county. Instead, the Albemarle counties appealed to the King as to whether the rump assembly had the right to limit the number of county delegates. At the same time Johnston appealed his side of the case of England.

The King and his council ignored the matter for seven years. Meanwhile, Johnston called thirteen sessions of the assembly, eleven of which met in New Bern, one in Bath, and one in Wilmington. Needless to say, the Albemarle was not represented.

To put it mildly, this led to a very confusing situation in the Albemarle region, which was on the verge of open revolt. Johnston himself wrote: "Tho' they do not appear in Arms, they are really in a State of Civil Rebellion." He did not see "how we can long keep up the face of Government." Quitrents and taxes were not paid, laws of the 1746 legislature were not obeyed, and the courts were openly disregarded. So bad was the situation that Bishop Augustus Spangenberg, the great Moravian leader, wrote that "first law" was about all that was left.

And so matters stood at the time of the death of Johnston. In fact, it was as not until two years later, in 1754, that the Privy Council solved the matter by disallowing the two 1746 laws. Thus the Albemarle side was upheld and the chaos caused by Johnston was smoothed out.

One of the things for which Johnston should be given great credit, however, was the great number of immigrants who poured into the province during his administration. They streamed in from western Europe—the Lowland Scots, the Highland Scots, and the Ulster Scots, the Irish, the Germans, the Welsh, and the Swiss. Particularly worthy of note were the large group of Highland Scots—the only large group to come to North Carolina directly from their native land rather than making their way via Pennsylvania, Virginia, or South Carolina. So pleased was this group with the Cape Fear valley that they petitioned the assembly in February, 1740: "If Proper encouragement be given them, they'll invite the rest of their friends and acquaintances over." The idea appealed to their Lowland brother Johnston, and he induced the assembly to exempt the newcomers from all taxation for ten years. Moreover, a similar exemption was offered to all Highlanders who came over in groups of forty or more. Johnston was also requested "to use his Interest . . . to obtain an Instruction for giving Encouragement to Protestants from foreign parts, to settle in Townships within this Province."

It is not too surprising that Johnston should have been extremely partial to the Highlanders. The news of their defeat by the English at Culloden Moor in Scotland in April, 1746, was met so coldly by Johnston that many suspected him of being disloyal to the king of England. And when he was shown a list of the Scottish "Rebel Chiefs" who had been killed or captured in the battle, he "exprest a concern for them saying many of them were his acquaintances and school fellows." Even more serious was the charge that he had shirked his duty in not ordering "Public rejoicings upon Advice of the most happy Defeat of the Rebels at Culloden." Equally serious was the charge that he had turned poor

German settlers from the Palatine section of Germany off their lands in Carolina in order to make room for the Scottish rebels.

Naturally the full extent of Johnston's responsibility for the increased number of immigrants coming over cannot be determined, but certainly he provided the newcomers with a hospitable welcome.

In addition to the above contributions, Johnston sought to encourage the development of the colony's commerce, industry, and agriculture and constantly stressed that North Carolina should provide the mother country with the raw materials and products which she so desperately needed for her livelihood. He particularly dreamed of getting the assembly to encourage—by the means of bounties or bonuses —the raising of mulberry trees for silk worms and the growing of grapes for wine, indigo for dye, flax for linen, and hemp for rope. In order to set an example he planted mulberry trees on his plantation, Brompton, near Elizabethtown in Bladen County. He was overjoyed when he made a crop of silk "truly bona fide on my own plantation."

In order to improve the quality and standards of North Carolina exports Johnston induced the assembly to pass a law for their inspection and by 1750 he noted a rise in the shipment of corn, peas, pork, beef, tobacco, wheat, rice, indigo, and potash.

Despite the delay in the payment of his salary, Johnston was able to amass a very sizable estate before his death. He had acquired some 25,000 acres of land and 103 slaves on farms in Granville, Tyrrell, Bertie, Northampton, Craven, and Bladen counties. Perhaps his pre-occupation with these personal affairs was the reason some of his administrative policies fell short of their goal.

Johnston first married Penelope Galland, step-daughter of the Proprietary Governor, Charles Eden. She was one of the wealthiest women of the province and was mistress of Eden House, just across the Chowan River from Edenton where Johnston made his home for a number of years. He and Penelope had a daughter who married John Dawson of Edenton. After his first wife's death, Johnston married Frances Butler. After his death, she married John Rutherford who was the tax receiver at Wilmington.

Johnston died in July 1752, but left little of his imprint on the early history of North Carolina. No known portrait

GOVERNOR JOHNSTON'S ARMORIAL BOOKPLATE

From his personal copy of *A Paraphrase and Comment Upon the Epistles and Gospels, Appointed to be Used in the Church of England* (London: 1726) by George Stanhope. This volume is now in the North Carolina Collection, University of North Carolina Library, Chapel Hill.

of him has come to light, though there are books in the University of North Carolina library with his bookmark. There is also some doubt as to the location of his grave which most records show to be in a grove of willows at Edenhouse Point, near his home there. Nevertheless, some Edenton residents contend that, since there is no marker, the records are wrong. The director of the North Carolina Collection at the University of North Carolina, William S. Powell, however, does not support this contention:

> I can find no evidence which would lead me to doubt that Gov. Johnston is buried at Eden House. The *Virginia Gazette* of July 24, 1752, reported his death there; I find many secondary sources which report that he is buried there; and a reference to his will in the Andrews' *Journal of a Lady of Quality* would seem to support this belief.

Perhaps the best summary of Johnson's contribution to the history of North Carolina was that written by Phillips Russell, biographer, historian, and retired professor of journalism at Chapel Hill. After pointing to Johnston's long administration of eighteen years, Professor Russell wrote:

> He had other distinctions. He saw North Carolina's population rise from less than 30,000 to 90,000. He saw the people spreading from the sea coast to the foot of the mountains. He saw the beginning of the great waves of immigration that profoundly affected the history of the colony and State. He virtually killed Brunswick as a port and set up Wilmington in its stead. He saw a sectional split between the Albemarle and Cape Fear areas. He encouraged the first law revisal and the first printery to be established within the province. He tried to make North Carolina a wine- and silk-producing country, with more attention to indigo, flax and hemp than pork and corn, and he had other useful ideas.

CHAPTER III

Arthur Dobbs
1754-1765

Few royal governors in all America had as distinguished a background of service to the British Empire as did Arthur Dobbs.

The Dobbs family—originally from England—had settled near Carrickfergus, in County Antrim, Ireland, as early as 1599. Here Arthur's great-great-grandfather built a small castle, from which the estate derived the name Castle Dobbs. And here it was that Arthur's father, Richard Dobbs, brought his wife in 1688, where the couple could manage the estate while Richard's father served as mayor of Carrickfergus. But because of the danger of an invasion of Ireland by the English forces, Richard sent his wife to Scotland where Arthur was born "on Tuesday morning being ye 2 of April 1689."

When peace returned and Ireland had been completely subjugated, Mary returned with her children to Castle Dobbs. On this pleasant estate Arthur romped with his brother Richard and two sisters, Jane and Elizabeth. Later, three half-sisters joined them, but by then Arthur was too old to engage in their frolics.

Unfortunately, there are no records pertaining to Dobbs' education. It is believed by his biographer, Desmond Clarke, however, that he received most of his education in England, but his name does not appear on the rolls at Oxford or Cambridge, or even at Dublin, Ireland. At any rate he was a well educated man, being both a good classical scholar and a scientist.

At the age of twenty-two, he purchased—as was the custom then—a cornetcy in a regiment of British dragoons, which would later be known as the Inniskilling Dragoons. After eighteen months of active duty in Scotland, he was placed on half pay status in October, 1712, where he remained for almost twenty years. In 1714 he returned to Ireland as the master of Castle Dobbs, "a moderately large and well-ordered estate," from which he derived a fairly good income.

In his thirtieth year Dobbs married Anne Osburn Northbury, a young widow whose large estate was added to that of her new husband. The following year, 1720, he began his political advancement by being appointed High Sheriff of Antrim, a position which brought him into contact with many influential people. He was next elected Mayor of Carrickfergus—a position which had been held by both his father and grandfather.

At this point in his career, Dobbs had made no great name for himself. His biographer described his situation as follows:

> Though Dobbs lived a fairly full and active life, showing a diversity of interests and tastes, he was very far from satisfied with the ordinary every day life of an eighteenth-century landlord. He was a restless, energetic, and ambitious man with all the ambitious man's love of power, authority, influence, and wealth. Despite his restless and ambitious nature, however, he had achieved little, and his prospects, at least in Ireland, were by no means good. Dobbs realized that the paths of ambitious Irishmen were strewn with many obstacles. Few important positions in State, Church, or Government were within reach of the average Protestant Irishman who lacked solid political backing and influence. Even a seat in Parliament seemed unobtainable, though in this respect Dobbs could count on a strong measure of support from the rather independent electors of Carrickfergus.

Normally, however, the patronage of a noble lord or the friendship of a borough patron paved the way to Parliament·

Up to his fortieth year, therefore, although acquiring some wealth and a little influence in his own country, he had attained no more responsible positions than those of High Sheriff of Antrim and Mayor of Carrickfergus.

Shortly afterwards he was appointed to the office of Deputy Governor of Carrickfergus by Carteret, the Lord Lieutenant of Ireland. This was an important step, because it brought him into close association with Lord Conway, one of the most influential men in Ireland and a relative of Sir Robert Walpole, the first prime minister of England. In token of Conway's friendship, Dobbs named his eldest son Conway Richard.

Through the support of Conway and other important public men, Dobbs was elected to the Irish Parliament in 1727 by a large majority, though the election—a long-drawn-out affair—cost him over £1,000. It was during this period that he published an important and penetrating book on Irish economic history, entitled *Essay on the Trade and Improvement of Ireland*. After making a survey of the political, social, and economic state of the country, he offered practical suggestions for increasing Irish trade, providing employment, and raising the standard of living of the people in general. But Dobbs felt that the real future of Ireland lay in abolishing the Irish Parliament and sending Irish delegates to the British Parliament in London—a plan far ahead of the times. He felt that by such a union Ireland would reap all the benefits of the Navigation Acts—or trade laws— just as Scotland did. Along this same line he advocated free trade and the abolition of such world trade barriers as tariffs and duties. This was a most far-sighted stand for an eighteenth-century observer in view of the present free trade agreement in the British Commonwealth of Nations and Britain's modern-day efforts to join the Common Market of Western Europe.

Dobbs also turned his inquiring mind towards Britain's rich American colonies, which were thorns in the flesh of France and Spain, who threatened to seize them at any moment. He prepared a long memorandum in which he set forth a more vigorous policy calling for the strengthening of their defenses. This memorandum was presented to Prime Minister Robert Walpole himself, and paved the way to an all-important meeting between the ambitious Irishman and the most influential man in England. Particularly interesting in the light of future events were Dobbs' suggestions in regard to the trade and development of the English colonies and his plans to push the French out of Canada.

Meanwhile, during 1731 and 1732, he played an active part in the Irish Parliament, serving on important committees and introducing progressive bills.

It was at this time, too, that Dobbs became fascinated by the idea of a Northwest Passage across North America to the Pacific Ocean—an idea that had long intrigued geographers and explorers. In his usual fashion he made a detailed study of the project and drew up a memorandum to the British authorities urging an immediate voyage of exploration before the French got the jump on them. This plan, too, was submitted to Walpole, who looked upon it and its author with favor. And this friendship with Walpole paid off when he appointed Dobbs His Majesty's Engineer and Surveyor-General of Ireland—a position of considerable importance.

Energetic pressure on Dobbs' part finally led to the sending by the Hudson Bay Company of two ships to the west coast of Hudson Bay to search for the passage. This voyage, of course, was fruitless, but it did not dampen Dobbs' ardor. He begged and pleaded continuously with the British Admiralty until finally, in May, 1741, two more ships of the British Navy were dispatched on the search. Again they returned without having found the desired passage, but this voyage did prove beyond a reasonable doubt that no such passage existed in the Hudson Bay region. And to Dobbs, according to his biographer,

> must go some of the credit for such success as this expedition achieved, for it was his initiative, his drive and energy that made it possible, and his efforts are imperishably enshrined in the northern cape of Hudson Bay that bears his name.

Not content with these two expeditions, however, Dobbs was able, through subscriptions, to send out still another two ships, which set sail in May, 1746, carrying with them the hopes and dreams of Arthur Dobbs. But though this expedition, too, led to no passage, Dobbs never gave up his belief in its existence.

In line with his adventuresome spirit—reminiscent of the great age of Elizabeth I—Dobbs had early shown an interest in the American colonies, as has been seen from his first memorandum to Sir Robert Walpole. In 1735 he approached a number of Government officials and large London merchants with a scheme to settle distressed Protestant families from Ireland in North Carolina. The idea had great appeal and Henry McCulloh, a great London merchant and kinsman of Governor Samuel Johnston of North Carolina, petitioned the Board of Trade for a tract of one- and a quarter-million acres at the headwaters of the Pee Dee, Cape Fear, and Neuse rivers in North Carolina. Dobbs' first real venture as a colonial proprietor did not come until 1745, when he and Colonel John Selwyn purchased from McCulloh and his associates a tract of 400,000 acres in what are now, roughly speaking, Mecklenburg and Cabarrus counties in North Carolina.

This grant, like others from the King, provided that the proprietor must settle one white person on every two hundred acres of the grant and that all unsettled land should revert to the Crown after ten years had elapsed. Therefore, Dobbs set to work at once to settle his newly acquired real estate. He immediately employed Matthew Rowan, the Surveyor-General and a native of County Antrim, to carry out a survey, and to supply him with full details as to such things as the number of acres and the produce. Dobbs' letters to Rowan, moreover, showed a surprising knowledge of the colony and its people.

While Rowan was busy on this side of the Atlantic, Dobbs lost no time in seeking out suitable families in his native Antrim and in offering them all types of inducements to try their fortunes on his lands in the New World. Even before he became governor of the colony, some five hundred people had settled on his lands.

Dobbs' interest in colonial ventures awakened in him a desire to become a colonial governor. His interest was further whetted by an invitation to join a group of English merchants and Virginia planters in a new project—the Ohio Company of Virginia. This land company, organized in 1748, proposed to secure a share of the Indian trade, to exploit and settle the Ohio Valley, an action that would bring to a climax the struggle between Britain and France for the possession, not only of the Ohio Valley, but for all North America. Dobbs was considered something of an outsider by such Virginia aristocrats as Thomas Lee, Thomas Cresap, and Lawrence Washington, but he played an important part in the formation of the company. In fact, he helped in preparing the petition to the King and exerted great influence among his friends to obtain the grant. The next year, 1749, the King granted the company 200,000 acres of land on the Ohio, and promised 300,000 more if the first grant was successfully settled. The importance of this company has been underestimated in American history. Certainly it was mainly responsible for the ultimate fate of the Ohio Valley— that it became British rather than French. Certainly it was a direct challenge to France and led to the final struggle between France and England for supremacy in the New World. And certainly Arthur Dobbs, who made no fortune in the venture, realized its significance when he later wrote:

> I thank God for sparing me so long among so many contemporaries, with health and money sufficient as to finish what I engage in, and live to see my long projected plan of driving the French out of the continent and I hope out of America . . . and what is a great addition to my pleasure is that I have been instrumental in so soon entering into this American war by my soliciting . . . the grant to the Ohio Company which was the means of bringing on the war before the French were prepared to begin their attack against our colonies.

Meanwhile, Dobbs was meeting with success persuading many families from northern Ireland to settle in his land in North America. He willingly paid the cost of transportation, and on one occasion, at least, he chartered a ship to take his settlers across the Atlantic. And despite his age, he himself was willing to make the perilous voyage across the Atlantic and take up an existence in the new land. He wrote his friend Matthew Rowan: "I still have hopes of visiting you in Carolina, and hope, if I keep my health, of fixing my affairs here with my son, so as to carry over my second son with me, by which time my friend Milhaus will have a lodge built where I can stay when I go over, till I am better provided with a house."

PORTRAIT OF DOBBS BY WILLIAM HOARE

As for his application for a governorship, the first known indication of this ambition appears in a letter of 1751 to George Selwyn:

> The favour you have always been pleased to show me . . . encourages me to apply to you for your . . . recommendation in an application I am making not only to serve myself but also to have it in my power to serve the government and British interests whilst I have health and strength to live an active life, which is for a government on the continent of America, where I could hope to be of service not only in promoting such improvements as might be useful to the British commerce, but also to extend our commerce into the continent by taking proper methods to instruct and civilize the natives . . . and so far strengthen our colonies against another war, as by our Indian allies we might secure the whole northern continent from the French . . .

Shortly after this letter was written, Governor Gabriel Johnston died, and Dobbs began to press his claims for the vacant governorship even more vigorously. Upon being assured of success he took a vacation at Bath, the famous English watering place, where he had his portrait painted by William Hoare, a fashionable artist of the period. Though Dobbs was sixty-three at the time, the portrait gives the impression of a younger man. His biographer comments that there is "considerable life and vigour about the portrait, which gives the impression of a tall, active man, austere and spartan in an age noted for the flabbiness of dissipation."

While waiting for his commission and the drafting of his instructions as Governor of North Carolina, Dobbs returned to Ireland, put his affairs in order, and settled his estates there on his son Conway. Still his instructions were delayed, but he was able to write his son on January 31, 1754, that his "French families is arrived at New Bern," and that he was securing additional colonists to come over. In fact, he wrote that he had a gentleman "who will undertake to send over annually 1,000 Palatines and Germans, one third of which will pay their own passage, or he will engage to carry them over at 20s. [shillings] a head, paid by the colony, so that we shall soon settle all our lands."

In addition to helping the Board of Trade draw up new instructions to all the colonial governors, Dobbs very wisely and prudently made provision for the future payment of his own salary. No doubt he had received wind of his predecessor's difficulties in this regard. He wrote that he had presented a memorial to the Treasury "for an appointment of my salary from this side, as the quitrents at present are just sufficient to pay the Establishment the cost of administration which is many thousand pounds in arrears." Therefore, unlike his predecessors, he would not be dependent upon the colonial assembly for his salary.

In the long wait in London he had continued to urge upon the Government the need for vigorous action against the French, who continued to press into the Ohio Valley. He also instructed the government in North Carolina to "repel force with force" and to build forts as defense measures.

At long last the British Government, realizing the grave French threat in America, instructed Dobbs, in early June, to proceed immediately to Spithead to join an armed convoy ready to depart. Forced to leave behind a number of settlers he had engaged, he boarded the *Garland* with only his son Edward and his nephew Richard Spaight, along with a few personal servants. After twelve weeks of foul weather, the convoy reached Hampton, Virginia, where he was met and escorted to Williamsburg by Governor Robert Dinwiddie.

They were joined there by Governor Horatio Sharpe of Maryland, and the three of them held a conference in which they tried to draw up united plans for defense against the French. Two days later Dobbs set sail for New Bern, where he arrived on October 31, 1754, and thus began, at the age of sixty-six, the most difficult task of his life.

Dobbs' appointment met with a certain amount of enthusiasm on the part of the people of North Carolina. Weary of strife and misgovernment, they welcomed the idea of some stability and order in government in the face of the impending war with France. Moreover, they knew that Dobbs was deeply interested in the social and economic advancement of the colony.

After Johnston's death in 1752, the office of Acting Governor had been assumed by Nathaniel Rice, President of the Council. A feeble old man, he died after six months and was succeeded by Matthew Rowan, who directed affairs with ability and vigor in the face of the now open war with France. This war, later called the French and Indian War in America, would develop two years later into a European conflict—and one on the high seas—which would be called the Seven Years War in Europe. More correctly, it should be called the Great War for Empire, because the fates of the British and French empires were at stake.

It must have been a great relief to have a duly empowered new governor, who brought direction and money, and the good news that a fully equipped army would sail from England in the spring. Dobbs had hardly arrived when he called a meeting of the assembly. In a statesmanlike address he outlined what he considered needed legislation for the advancement of the colony, dealing with the promotion of trade and industry, Indian affairs, etc. He then turned to the most important matter—defense—in which he argued that we "are not to be intimidated or bullied out of our rights" by the French.

The address was well received by the assembly and was followed by a harmonious session. The legislators appropriated a large sum to pursue the war against France and to raise troops for the defense of Virginia. They further carried out the governor's recommendations by passing laws regulating the payment of quitrents, providing for an improved court system, and for a Vestry Act which divided the colony into parishes and led to a stronger Established Church in the colony.

The promised British forces—commanded by General Edward Braddock—arrived in New York early in 1775. North Carolina sent a small force there with Edward Dobbs, the governor's son, in charge to join Braddock. In addition, young Hugh Waddell was sent to superintend the building of Fort Dobbs (near present-day Statesville) on what was then considered the frontier of the colony.

From the very start Dobbs devoted his untiring energies to the welfare of the colony. And when the first session of the assembly finished on January 15, 1755, he could report that it had been harmonious and co-operative in every way. He then turned to a more detailed study of th colony and decided that there were two pressing problems: the needs for a permanent and more suitable capital, and for a series of forts for protection.

Feeling that neither New Bern nor Wilmington was adequate for the seat of government, he set out on a trip up the Neuse River in search of a proper and more central location. Near the present town of Kinston (or Kingston, as it was originally called), he found the site, Tower Hill, he desired and promptly bought up the necessary land for the colonial government. Later the assembly made the necessary appropriation, but it was disallowed in England.

Dobbs set out on a sloop to survey the coastline minutely and to decide on proper locations for forts and coastal defenses. He was most impressed with the possibilities of a fine port and fort at Cape Lookout, but his suggestions were never carried out. He followed up this cruise by a tedious journey into piedmont North Carolina. In a detailed account, he described his trip up the Yadkin River, to the newly-established town of Salisbury, and on the the western limit of the Granville line and to the northwest corner of his own vast estate. Here he was warmly received by Ulster Scots, Germans, and Swiss, whom he described as follows:

> There are at present 75 families on my lands. I viewed betwixt 30 and 40 of them, and except two there were not less than from 5 or 6 to 10 children in each family, each going barefooted in their shifts in the warm weather, no woman wearing more than a shift and one thin petticoat; they are a colony from Ireland removed from Pennsylvania, of what we call Scotch Irish Presbyterians, who with others in their neighboring tracts settled together in order to have a teacher of their own opinion. Besides these there are 22 families of Germans or Swiss, who are all an industrious people, they raise horses, cows and hogs with a few sheep; they raise Indian corn, wheat, barley, rye and oats, and make good butter and tolerable cheese, which they sell at Charlestown, having a waggon road to it, tho' 200 miles distant.

Dobbs reached New Bern again in mid-August after a trip that would have exhausted many a younger and less energetic man. This trip in itself certainly refutes the oft-repeated statement that he was old and anile when he was appointed govenor.

While near Salisbury, Dobbs had received news of the tragic defeat of General Braddock's forces on the Monongahela. Therefore, when the assembly met in September, 1765, Dobbs, acutely aware of the defenselessness of the colony, urged the members to take all possible aid to carry out a defense program. Nor did he neglect the internal affairs of the province, but pointed to the great need for the revisal of laws, the erection of county or parish schools, and the proper treatment of the Indians.

The assembly, accordingly, granted £10,000 to raise three companies of soldiers and £7,500 for the purchase of glebes (rectors' houses) and for the erection of churches and public buildings. Before any further business could be transacted, the governor and one-third of the members had become "very sickly with Agues and intermittent fever," and Dobbs was forced to send them home. But he was pleased over the appointment—upon his recommendation—of his son Edward and his nephew, Richard Spaight, as members of his Council.

Throughout the year 1756 affairs of a domestic nature gave Dobbs little concern. In fact, a spirit of harmony and good-will prevailed throughout the province. But there was grave concern over the progress of the war, in which the French had the upper hand.

Meanwhile, the Earl of Loundoun had been sent over as Commander-in-Chief to succeed Braddock, and in February, 1757, he called a meeting of the governors of Virginia, Maryland, Pennsylvania, and North Carolina to meet in Philadelphia. Against a background of much pomp and ceremony, and dinners and banquets, they devised a purely defensive campaign. Dobbs, on behalf of North Carolina, agreed to raise two hundred men for the defense of North Carolina, and another two hundred to be sent to South Carolina, which appeared to be the target of an early French attack. To the credit of Dobbs, the assembly carried out his pledge and made the necessary appropriations.

However, by the end of the year 1757 there appeared the first rift between Dobbs and his assembly. Because of the inefficient administration of the land office, the unsatisfactory state of the quitrent collection, and the neglect in collecting taxes due the government, Dobbs removed from office John Rutherford, the Receiver General of the province, and James Murray, the Attorney General. Though Dobbs was accused by some of being hot-tempered, his actions were approved by the Board of Trade in London. Dobbs did what no previous governor had done when he laid his instructions from the Board before the assembly for them to see what a difficult role he had to play, thus preventing for a time an open rift between the governor and his assembly.

The year 1758 brought with it marked success for British forces in the New World. A new spirit had been breathed into their cause by the energy and vision of William Pitt. Nor was this year uneventful for Dobbs. Rutherford and Murray, whom he had dismissed, continued to raise opposition to the governor. Rutherford even appealed his case to the Earl of Granville, charging that it was "well known that the understanding & Judgment of the Governor is wasted and greatly impaired, and also how much he is guided by his countrymen residing in this province and determined to elbow out anybody in Place of Trust to make room for them."

The Board of Trade, rather than reopening the case, censured Rutherford for his appeal; but this action tended to strengthen opposition to the governor in the assembly. And from this time until his death there would be charges that he was too hotheaded, anile, and guilty of nepotism (or favoritism to his family). While Dobbs' hotheadedness was undeniably true, his mind was as clear as a bell, and his only act of nepotism was granting seats on his Council to his son and nephew, the latter of whom was secretary to the governor and of the province.

Having been unsuccessful in establishing a permanent seat of government at Tower Hill on the Neuse, and finding New

Bern too humid for his rheumatism, Dobbs purchased a residence at Brunswick, to which he moved in 1758. Here he had already encouraged the construction of St. Philip's Church, which was designated as His Majesty's Chapel in the province. A special pew, raised above the others, was set aside for the governor. This move, however, was probably a mistake, since it set him apart from many of his older friends and he became, according to his biographer, "a little more impatient, petulant, and, at times, irascible."

English success in driving the French from America brought an increased spirit of independence throughout colonial America. And by 1759 North Carolinians were experiencing a spirit of unrest and dissatisfaction with British rule. A drawn-out war had saddled them with debt; internal affairs had been neglected; Indian warriors were a menace on the frontier; the existence of the Granville district, "a state within a state"—all served to create a condition of discontent and uneasiness. Particularly pressing was the question of the oppression of Lord Granville's agents which led to the outbreak of riots in Edgecombe County and elsewhere.

The assembly charged the governor with failure to put down the riots, thus tending to widen the breach between the two. Harmonious relations were further strained when the King-in-Council disallowed a number of bills passed by the assembly. Among these were acts for the establishment of higher and lower courts, and for the setting up of vestries and the payment of salaries to orthodox clergy. Relations were also strained when Dobbs vetoed a bill appointing an agent to represent the colony in London—principally because it was tacked on as a rider to an Aid bill.

The Aid bill was the result of an urgent appeal from William Pitt to Dobbs for further aid in men and money to bring the war to an end. The assembly promptly responded with such a bill, but tacked on a number of riders, including the above-mentioned one. When the assembly refused to strike out the riders, Dobbs prorogued it.

Before going home, however, the assembly, over the head of governor, appointed an agent in London to represent its interests—a highly irregular action in the eyes of the governor.

At the meeting of the next assembly, both governor and assembly were in a more conciliatory mood, perhaps because of the momentous event of the fall of Quebec to the British. Dobbs' address showed a real desire to heal old wounds; the assembly promised to avoid inserting any more riders. But a better understanding was soon broken when the assembly passed a bill for the issuance of paper money to pay the troops and carry on the government. Dobbs, following instructions from England, refused to sign it, and once again he and the assembly were at loggerheads. Dobbs, therefore, dissolved the assembly in January, 1760, and ordered new elections, hoping for a more friendly body of new delegates.

The new assembly, which met in April, was even less conciliatory and, after many serious disputes, resolved itself into a secret committee of the whole to draw up a list of charges against the governor to be sent to the King. The long list included serious charges of widespread maladministration, misappropriation of funds, nepotism, and oppressive rule which trampled on the just rights of the people. These charges were grossly exaggerated and were ignored by the English authorities, but they do indicate something of the temper of the people. Certainly, in the bitter squabbles between the two, neither side was blameless and neither side tried to restrain its temper. In the final analysis, the governor was trying to carry out his instructions from England and uphold the royal prerogative; the assembly was trying to assert and maintain its rights and privileges as an elective body whose powers, it felt, were co-equal with those of the English Parliament.

When the next assembly met in November, 1760, Dobbs was able to report "the Glorious Conquest and Acquisition of all Canada" by the British. He hoped now to be able to promote the economic and social progress of the province. But another call for an Aid bill to bring about an end to Indian fighting prompted the assembly to add on another clause appointing an agent in London. Again Dobbs vetoed the bill and was censured by the Board of Trade for so doing. No doubt because of this censure, in the next session he approved an Aid bill with the tacked-on appointment of an agent in London.

Meanwhile, George II had died in October, 1760, and was succeeded by George III, who at once confirmed Dobbs as governor and sent along additional instructions and increased powers.

At this point Dobbs, now seventy-two years old, was able to turn to his personal affairs for a period. Though he was beset with problems, such as the lawlessness along the unsettled South Carolina border and the refusal of the assembly to enact another Aid bill, Dobbs spent a comparatively quiet time, relatively free from criticism, that is, until, in the fall of 1762, he married a fifteen-year-old girl. This marriage, in St. Philip's Church at Brunswick, of the seventy-three year old governor to Justina Davis subjected him to an avalanche of ridicule and lampoonery. Yet to all appearances his young wife was happy and she was a solace to him in his old age.

A few months later he suffered a stroke of paralysis which left his lower limbs almost useless, though he continued to attend meetings of his Council and to carry on the required business of state. His health did not improve and he was forced to resort to a wheelchair. He was, moreover, greatly depressed over the death of his nephew and secretary, Richard Spaight. The latter left a son, Richard Dobbs Spaight, who would become the eighth governor of the independent State of North Carolina.

In the spring Dobbs' health improved to such an extent that he was able to get around with a cane and to make a trip all the way to Augusta, Georgia. There he and the governors of South Carolina and Georgia drew up a treaty of peace and alliance with the six Indian nations of the southeastern area.

The following spring, after ten years of service, Dobbs wrote to Lord Halifax, requesting a leave of absence to return to England. The request was granted, and Colonel William Tryon was sent over as lieutenant-governor to administer the government during Dobbs' absence.

Dobbs, whose health steadily improved, and his young wife, who eagerly looked forward to the trip, began making plans to join his son Conway in northern Ireland. He set his time of departue for the spring of 1765. This plan, plus his anouncement that he would not relinquish his office till then, greatly upset the ambitious young Tryon, who was chafing at the bit to assume his duties.

Dobbs' last assembly met that fall in Wilmington. Before adjourning, the Council (which was the upper house) tendered him "its unfeigned and grateful acknowledgment" for his labors. The Commons (which was the lower house) was more restrained, but it did wish him "a pleasant voyage and a safe arrival in Britain, and that your native air may have all those salutary effects for the re-establishment of your health that you can wish."

After the prorogation of the assembly, Dobbs returned to his plantation, Russellborough, near Brunswick, to prepare for his departure. But about a week before he was to sail he had a severe seizure while packing. Two days later, on March 28th, he died in his wife's arms.

Dobbs was buried in Brunswick at St. Philip's Church, which he had been respsonsible for establishing. Today there are no visible remains of his grave.

CHAPTER IV

William Tryon
1765-1771

William Tryon, the fourth royal governor of North Carolina, was born the very year—1729—that North Carolina became a royal colony. He was thus thirty-six years old when he arrived at Brunswick.

Tryon was the son of Charles Tryon of "Bulwick", Northamptonshire, England, and Lady Mary Tryon. Her father was the first Earl of Ferrers and she was the sister of Sewallis Shirley, Comptroller to the Royal Household. It is assumed that young Tryon grew up on the family estate, Norbury Park in Surrey, which he sold when he came to North Carolina. His ancestry could be traced back directly to the Earl of Essex, a favorite of Queen Elizabeth I, and to the royal house of Plantagenet.

At the age of twenty-eight Tryon became a captain in the First Regiment of Footguards and shortly afterwards was married. His bride was an heiress, Margaret Wake, of fashionable Hanover Street, London, who brought him a dowry of £30,000. Young Mistress Tryon also had the advantage of being a relative of the President of the Board of Trade, Lord Hillsborough, who later held the important position of Secretary of State for the Colonies from 1767 to 1772. The young lieutenant-governor thus had wealth, position, and influential connections when he arrived in North Carolina on October 11, 1764.

Accompanying him was his wife, their four-year-old daughter, Margaret, and Lady Tryon's cousin, Fountain Elwin, who was Tryon's secretary. Also with them was a servant from Norfolk and John Hawks, whom Tryon described as "a very able worthy master builder," who would later prove his merit as the architect of Tryon Palace.

No sooner had Tryon arrived, eager to take over his new duties, than he was informed by the aged and feeble, but still redoubtable, Governor Arthur Dobbs that the latter did not intend to relinquish his office until the following spring. This struck Tryon like a "thunderbolt," as he described it. He further complained in a letter to Lord Halifax that among his "lesser disappointments is the want of a house, as the Governor has declined letting me his villa till his departure." Dobbs however did offer the Tryons the hospitality of his home, "Castle Dobbs," near Brunswick.

The Tryons rented a house in Wilmington to be used during meetings of the Land Office, a house in New Bern to be used when the assembly met there, and a "villa" about three miles from New Bern. Then two months after the death of Governor Dobbs, which occurred March 28, 1765, the new governor purchased "Castle Dobbs" at Russellborough, which soon became known as "Castle Tryon." Here the Tryons lived most of the time until his new palace in New Bern was completed.

The Tryons had hardly settled themselves in the province when they, along with Fountain Elwin, set out on a five-hundred-mile tour of eastern North Carolina. They chose mid-December, because of the heat and the fear of fever in summer. But a rough and tedious trip it must have been! The roads were impossible and, especially in the up-country, virtually impassable and were little more than trading paths, Rivers, swamps, and fallen trees added to the hazards.

From Brunswick the Tryon party made a slow progress—presumably in a chariot—up to New Bern (founded in 1710) on the Trent River, to Bath (founded in 1705), on the

Pamlico, and to Edenton (the capital of the province from 1720 to 1738) overlooking Albemarle Sound. From Edenton they journeyed north as far as the Virginia line and then proceeded seventy miles west to Halifax, the political and trading center on the Roanoke River. After a twenty-mile trip up stream to the falls of the river, they turned south, passing through Tarborough on their way to Wilmington. During the trip, which consumed two months, Tryon had hoped "to acquire a tolerable insight into the temper and genius of the inhabitants" of the province over which he would preside.

But this tour, through an area inhabited largely by an English population, could hardly give him the insight he desired. It would be two more years before he and his wife would travel into the up-country—to Campbellton and Cross Creek (later renamed Fayetteville), to Orange Court House (now Hillsboro), to Salisbury (the county seat of Rowan County), to Charlotte (then recently established as the seat of Mecklenburg), and to the Moravian settlements of Bethabara and Bethania (most of the inhabitants of which would move over to a newer town, Salem).

Throughout the piedmont they encountered a population far different from that of the English Anglicans and Quakers of the coastal plain. Here he found the Highland Scots (largely in the Cape Fear Valley) and the Ulster Scots, or Scotch-Irish, both of whom were Presbyterians. Here also he found Germans who were Moravians, Lutherans, and German Reformed. And it would be these non-English and non-Anglicans, whom he least understood, who soon would rise up against him in a revolt known as the War of the Regulation, or the Regulators' War.

If Tryon failed to understand the temper of these people, his tour of eastern North Carolina at least confirmed his intention of locating the capital at New Bern. Up till then it had met in various places—Edenton, Bath, New Bern, and Wilmington—depending on the whim of the governor. Dobbs, as we have seen, had tried unsuccessfully to fix a permanent capital forty miles up the Neuse, at Tower Hill, near present Kinston, but this recommendation had been disallowed in England.

Shortly after Dobbs' death, Tryon called his first assembly to meet in New Bern on May 2, 1765. But this session was destined to be short-lived. The members had hardly convened when news of the passage of the Stamp Act by the mother country reached New Bern. The immediate response in America was the calling of a Stamp Act Congress to meet in New York. All the colonial assemblies were requested to send delegates to combine their efforts to bring about its hasty repeal by the British government. North Carolina delegates, however, were not among those present in New York, because Tryon promptly prorogued the assembly on May 18th before they could elect delegates to attend and refused to reconvene it until after the repeal of the Stamp Act.

Tryon's earlier biographer described this action as "one of the shrewdest acts of Tryon's administration" and described Tryon as "a man of strong determination" who "bent every energy to carry out the decrees of Parliament." But later the lower house of the assembly, when it was finally reconvened in November 1766, after the repeal of the Stamp Act, took a dim view of the action. It officially informed the governor of its resentment of his action.

In all fairness it should be said that Tryon actually did not favor the Stamp Act, because it would drain the colony of its money. On the other hand, as long as it was the law, he was determined to uphold it with all the force at his command.

As is well known, the people were indignant over the Stamp Act. At this point they conceded the right of Parliament to levy a tax or tariff on external articles, or goods shipped into the colonies from England. But they greatly resented a tax on internal articles, such as newspapers, college diplomas, and all legal and commercial papers within the colony. As a result, demonstrations were held that summer and fall at New Bern, Edenton, Cross Creek, and Wilmington.

Tryon himself tried to overcome the resistance movement and to prepare the leading merchants of the Cape Fear area for the arrival of the stamps by inviting fifty of them to a dinner at "Castle Tryon." He even offered personally to pay the duty on tavern licenses and on many legal documents on which the new act levied a tax. But he had not reckoned on the temper of his guests. They steadfastly refused to be a party to any such deal. Moreover, three or four hundred patriots, organized as the "Sons of Liberty" (as they were known elsewhere up and down the Atlantic), with flags flying and drums beating, escorted the Stamp Master, William Houston, to the courthouse in Wilmington. Here he was forced to sign his own resignation on November 16, 1765.

In the following months other instances of complete defiance of Tryon and the King took place. Finally on February 21, 1766, a large body of these aroused "Sons of Liberty" surrounded Castle Tryon. Their leaders, Cornelius Harnett, sometimes called the "Father of the Revolution in North Carolina," demanded of Tryon that the Comptroller of the Port of Brunswick, William Pennington, be required to come outside. Tryon refused. Harnett looked the governor in the eye and declared that the people would take Pennington by force if necessary. Pennington, however, signified his willingness to resign, whereupon Tryon contemptuously put pen and paper before the official and ordered his resignation. "Now, Sir," said the governor, "you may go!" Thus no stamps were ever sold in North Carolina.

And thus also the "Sons of Liberty," composed of the planters and merchants of the Cape Fear, had preserved their liberties in an organized, orderly, and successful resistance. According to Professor Hugh T. Lefler, in no other colony was the resistance by force "so well organized and executed." It was resistance such as this, plus the protests of British shippers, that led to the repeal of the Stamp Act later in the same year. On June 25 Tryon issued a proclamation which formally announced repeal of the act. In their great joy the people overlooked the Declaratory Act, passed at the same time. By this act, Britain "declared" she had the right to tax the colonies in any way she saw fit. It would be on this issue, which gave rise to the principle of "no taxation without representation," that the War for Independence would be fought nine years later.

With the repeal of the hated Stamp Act and the reconvening of the assembly, Tryon decided that now was the right time to ask for an appropriation for the construction of public buildings which would fix the capital, presumably at New Bern. Certainly Tryon was justified in requesting a permanent capital. This position was also taken by James Davis, public printer and editor of the colony's first newspaper, the *North Carolina Gazette, who wrote:*

> Can you see the PUBLIC RECORDS Carted from Place to Place, and your Properties and Estates trusted to the mercy of a Shower of Rain, and at the Discretion of a Cart-Driver? Forbid it Heaven!

The assembly, in a magnanimous mood, appropriated £5,000 for the erection of the necessary buildings and authorized Tryon to purchase twelve lots for their location.

A tract of land was acquired in New Bern for the purpose. John Hawks, who had accompanied Tryon over from England, where he had been a surveyor of St. Paul's Cathedral in London, was the designer and builder of the new government buildings. The entire unit, which came to be known as Tryon Palace, would serve as the governor's residence, the meeting-place of the assembly and council, and as a repository for neglected public records.

The building which emerged, according to Alonzo T. Dill, the historian of Tryon Palace, "excited controversy by its heavy cost, bloodshed by its symbolization of royal authority's abuse, and admiration by its excellence of proportion, design, and setting."

As to the heavy cost, an additional £10,000 was appropriated in 1767, running the total up to £15,000. This amount was to be derived from a tax of two pence a gallon on all imported wine, rum, and distilled liquors, obtained from any place except Great Britain, and from a poll tax of eight pence proclamation money for the next two years. The next year an additional poll tax of two shillings was levied for three years. These measures, of course, imposed a real burden of the tax-laden citizens, particularly those in the piedmont. Typical of their reaction were the words of an irate man from Mecklenburg who wrote that "not one man in twenty of the four most populous counties [Orange, Rowan, Mecklenburg, and Anson] will even see this famous house when built, as their connections and trade do, and even will more naturally center in South Carolina." Another westerner wrote that they wanted no such building and would absolutely refuse to pay the tax, while another pointed out that a man worth £10,000 paid no more than a poor backwoodsman trying to eke out an existence. It can, therefore, easily be seen how the attempt to collect this unequal tax added greatly to the unrest in the piedmont.

Work was begun on the Palace in 1767. The plan called for an imposing central brick house of two main stories, with two wings of two low stories each, connected with the main building by semicircular colonnades. Many considered the structure, which was completed in 1770, as the handsomest government house in English America.

By the middle of 1770 the Tryons moved into the central building, though the two wings were not completed. And in December the assembly first met there. The formal opening was described by the *Virginia Gazette:*

> At Noon a Royal Salute was fired from the Battery, and in the Evening his Excellency gave a very grand and noble Entertainment and Ball at the Palace, at which were present the Honourable his Majesty's Council of this Province, the House of Assembly, a very great Number of Gentlemen and Ladies from different Parts of the Country, and the principal Gentlemen and Inhabitants of this Town. About eight in the Evening the Company were entertained with a very grand and surprising Exhibition of Fireworks . . . ; a Bonfire was also lighted up, and great Plenty of Liquor given to the Populace.

The new taxes for the construction of the Palace were not the only complaints of the people of the piedmont. Among the political grievances were gross under-representation in the assembly, by which the piedmont counties had only seventeen delegates to sixty-one for the other counties. And, during Tryon's rule, the governor, every councillor, every judge, the treasurer, and the speaker of the House lived in the East. Equally undemocratic was the character of local government, which was run by the county court. This court, which controlled almost every aspect of local government and administration, consisted of the justices of the peace sitting together. The latter were all appointed by the governor, and they in turn recommended to the governor the appointment of all local officials (the sheriff, constables, road overseers, etc.) except the clerk of the court, who was appointed by a royal official. Since two-thirds of the members of the assembly were also justices of the peace, there developed a very powerful and unhealthy "courthouse ring." Aggravating the situation even further was the system of multiple officeholding, by which one man could hold a number of public offices.

There were also a number of economic abuses, which were resented by the people of the piedmont. As early as June, 1765, a schoolmaster, George Sims, drew up a pamphlet called "The Nutbush Address" in which he described such injustices as excessive taxes, high rents, extortionate fees charged by county officials, and the fraudulent accounting of public funds.

Fired by this document and other outcries, a mass meeting of irate men assembled at Sandy Creek in Orange County in August, 1766, and issued a document called "Regulator Advertisement Number 1." It called for all the people of the province to put an end to local oppression. But the county officials of Orange and the assembly turned a deaf ear to their demands.

Insult was added to injury—in the minds of the backwoodsmen—when Governor Tryon, with a retinue of about a hundred, and at a cost of £1,490, marched all the way up to the Cherokee country to look into the running of the line between North Carolina and the Indian country. This expedition, which Tryon led from May 18 to June 13, was condemned as a "pompous, ridiculous, unnecessary and wasteful expenditure" of public funds in peace time.

Still seeking peaceful redress for their grievances, despite the cold shoulder from Tryon, the abused citizens, who now were called "Regulators," drew up another document, "Regulator Advertisement Number 6." This protest clearly set forth what abuses it authors sought to "regulate" and marks the formal organization of the movement. Its supporters solemnly agreed: (1) To pay no more taxes until they were satisfied that they were agreeable to law; (2) to pay no more fees than the laws required; (3) to subscribe to a fund for defraying necessary expenses; (4) to meet as often as they conveniently could; and (5) to allow a simple majority to rule in case of differences.

Tryon himself was certainly not unaware of the Regulators' grievances. He even admitted in a letter back home that "The Sheriffs have embezzled more than one-half of the public money ordered to be raised and collected by them . . . [about 40,000 pounds] . . . not 500 of which will possibly ever come into the Treasury."

Then, in the summer of 1768, Tryon was personally presented with "Regulator Advertisement Number 8" by Rednap Howell, known as the poet of the Regulation, and James Hunter, one of its leaders. After an apology to Tryon for anything that might be construed as derogatory to the King, the petition asked for redress for the abuses of corrupt men who occupied public office. Tryon took the complaints to his council and returned with the statement that the grievances did not justify the petitioners' violent course of action in refusing to pay their taxes. He gave them a direct order to give up the name of Regulators, to cease their organized activities, and to pay their taxes. Yet it must be said that he issued a warning to officials against charging excessive fees, ordered a list of legal fees to be charged, and directed the attorney general to bring to trial any officers or lawyers charged with extortion. He also promised to journey up to Hillsborough, the center of the troubles, in July, where he hoped to find everything peaceful.

None of this impressed Herman Husband, one of the Regulator leaders, who later said that Tryon was "inclined to the other side, multiplying all our faults to the highest pitch he was capable of."

True to his word, the governor did arrive in Hillsborough on July 6, but at the head of a large troop. He immediately ordered all public officials to post their legal fees and he demanded the collection of taxes for 1767. He then sought to provide for an orderly session of the Superior Court which in September was to try Herman Husband and William Butler, arrested on charges of "inciting the populace to rebellion."

Meanwhile, reports and rumors were flying back and forth. Tryon heard that the Regulators were gathering in a large body, and the Regulators heard that Tryon would attack them with his militia and would encourage the Cherokees to attack them from the rear. Tryon, however, met with a committee of the Regulators and assured them that he had no intention of inciting the Cherokees, and that the milita would not be sent against the Regulators if they remained at home. He also assured them that his henchman, Edmund Fanning, would be brought to trial at the September court on charges of extortion. Fanning, incidentally, has been described as the best educated but most hated man in the entire province. That hatred was reciprocated by him as he went about his duties as a multiple officeholder, serving as a lawyer, a member of the assembly, registrar, superior court judge, and colonel of the militia.

Between the middle of August and the middle of September, Tryon made a circuit of Orange, Rowan, and Mecklenburg counties. Here he reviewed what troops there were and conferred with the officers of the militia. With more threats of troubles in Hillsborough and reports that a thousand Regulators had assembled within twenty miles of Hillsborough, Tryon called out the militia to march with him from Salisbury to Hillsborough. Some eight hundred volunteered to join him—no mean feat in the back country. At Hillsborough he was joined by the Orange and Granville volunteer militia, which made up a total of 1,461 troops. This action cost the colony £5,000 and served to infuriate the Regulators.

Meanwhile some 3,700 Regulators—according to Husband—had gathered outside Hillsborough. The situation was tense, but all turned out peaceably. The Regulators sent a committee with an humble address to Tryon in which they asked for pardon and pledged that they would seek redress for their grievances only through legal means. The governor and his Council granted the pardon on condition that the Regulators promise to pay their taxes, surrender their arms, and deliver up nine leaders for trial. The upshot was that they made no promise, delivered up no leaders, and only thirty gave up their arms. Instead, they quietly returned home and the threatened "Battle of the Eno" (the river near Hillsborough) did not materialize.

Nor did the anxiously awaited September trials provoke any incidents. Husband was miraculously acquitted, and Butler and two others were fined only £50 and sentenced to six months imprisonment, but these three were pardoned by Tryon. Fanning was convicted of taking a six-shilling fee for registering a deed when the legal fee was two shillings and eight pence. He was fined one penny, and the cost of court. He promptly resigned, but this action did not appease the Regulators.

The next year of 1769 promised more hope for their cause when Tryon issued the long-awaited call for a new election to the assembly. When the ballots were counted in July, Orange, Anson, Granville and Halifax counties had returned solid Regulator delegations. Among them were none other than Herman Husband and Thomas Person, of Granville, considered "the brains of the Regulation," These men promptly and eagerly presented their grievances to the assembly, but Tryon, after only four days, dissolved it, pleading other issues for his action. Again the hopes of the Regulators were dashed by Tryon.

In the face of such rebuffs and disappointments, there is little wonder that the whole movement mushroomed. Disorders spread to Edgecombe, Anson, and Johnston counties. And in Hillsborough mob rule took over. On September 24 and 25, some 150 Regulators stormed into the courthouse where they assaulted a lawyer, dragged Fanning through the streets, and forced Judge Richard Henderson to flee. The following day a mock court was held in which

In the face of this renewed insult, Tryon hastily convened the assembly and urged them to adopt measures to meet the situation. The assembly responded with the Johnston Riot Act, by which prosecutions for riots might be tried in any county (whether they occurred there or not) and authorized the governor to use military force against the Regulators. The latter were now in a mood to meet force with force. In Rowan and Orange counties they passed resolutions promising to pay no more taxes, declaring Fanning an outlaw, forbiding any court sessions, and threatening to kill all lawyers and judges.

A lesser man than Tryon would probably have ducked the issue and have proceeded to New York, of which colony he had been appointed governor. But instead Tryon took

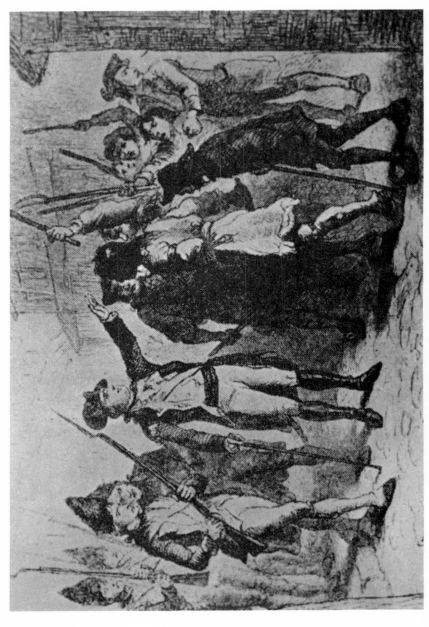

GOVERNOR TRYON AND THE REGULATORS IN ONE OF THEIR STORMY MEETINGS

drastic action. He immediately issued orders for a special term of court to convene in March, 1771, in Hillsborough, and called out the entire colonial militia to march there to protect the court and suppress the Regulators once and for all.

The response of the militia attests to Tryon's prestige. The Easterners marching with him numbered 1,068, and they were joined by enough men from Orange, Rowan, and a few other western counties to total 1,452 strong. Tryon's forces encamped on Great Alamance Creek, a few miles west of Hillsborough on May 16. Opposing him was a force of about 2,000 Regulators. Their leaders petitioned Tryon for an audience, but he refused as long as they remained under arms. He gave them exactly one hour in which to disperse and when they refused, he gave the order to fire.

In the ensuing battle—which lasted about two hours— the Regulators were soundly beaten and scattered. Each side lost nine killed. Sixty-one of Tryon's men were wounded; an undetermined number of the Regulators were wounded and fifteen were taken prisoner.

Tryon marched his troops back to Hillsborough, arriving on June 14. The prisoners were tried and twelve were sentenced to be hanged, but Tryon pardoned six of them. Regulator resistance had been crushed by Tryon, but some of their principles were later incorporated in the first Constitution of North Carolina in 1776.

Tryon, eager to leave for his new post in New York, returned ahead of his troops to New Bern, arriving June 26, where he was welcomed by a mass demonstration. Four days later the Tryons, accompanied by Edmund Fanning as his secretary, set sail for New York.

In that colony Tryon continued his energetic, progressive activities—strengthening the militia, founding New York

Hospital, extending the postal service, and other worthy projects. But, in the midst of these activities, misfortune struck. On December 29, 1773—at night while the entire household was asleep—fire completely destroyed the governor's mansion and all his possessions, and he and his family barely escaped with their lives.

In April, 1774, in weakened health as a result of growing tensions in the colony, Tryon sailed for England and did not return until June 28, 1775, after the battles of Lexington and Concord. And by October he had to seek refuge on board one of the British warships in New York harbor—where he fretted away his time until Sir William Howe recaptured the city on September 15, 1776.

Tryon's one great moment of glory in the Revolution came April 25-27, 1777, when he landed some 2,000 troops at what is now Westport, Connecticut, and burned the Whig supply depot at Danbury. For dealing such a blow to the Whigs he was promoted to colonel of the 70th (Surrey) Foot and was awarded the rank of major general "in America."

After the war shifted to the South, Tryon's role diminished and his health again declined. Racked with gout, he returned to England in 1780. He was promoted to lieutenant general in 1782. He died on January 27, 1788, at his home on Upper Grosvenor Street, London.

CHAPTER V

Josiah Martin
1771-1775

Josiah Martin was the last royal governor of North Carolina. His family could be traced back to the Norman Conquest of 1066, when one Martin of Tours came across the English Channel with William the Conqueror. Josiah Martin's own grandfather, Samuel, left England in the seventeenth century and settled on the island of Antigua in the West Indies. Samuel's son, also named Samuel, married Sarah Wyke, and it was to this couple that Josiah Martin was born on April 3, 1737. His childhood was far from lonely as he was surrounded by twenty-two brothers and sisters.

At the age of twenty, in 1757, young Martin entered the British Army as a commissioned officer. Four years later he was apparently stationed in New York, because in 1761 he married his cousin, Elizabeth, the daughter of another Josiah Martin, who resided at a country seat called "Rockhall" on Long Island, New York. Josiah and Elizabeth had eight children. After twelve years of service in the army, he resigned his commission as lieutenant colonel. He gave the reason as ill health, though he would live for seventeen more years apparently in normal health. And certainly the years he devoted to the governorship of North Carolina and to fighting during the Revolution were far more strenuous than the peace time army life he had previously led.

At the time he was commissioned by His Royal Majesty, George III, as governor of North Carolina early in 1771, Martin was in New York. Before departing to assume his duties, he conferred with William Tryon, his predecessor as governor of North Carolina, now governor of New York. Would that there were a record of Tryon's comments on affairs in North Carolina in the turbulent years of the Regulator troubles and the approach of the American Revolution!

The voyage from New York to North Carolina consumed nineteen days. Upon his arrival at New Bern, Martin and his family were established in the still-new and magnificent Tryon Palace overlooking the Trent River. He took the oath of his new office on August 12, 1771, little realizing, perhaps, what was in store for him.

The new governor was received by the citizens of the province in a friendly way, probably because of the reports of his amiable and pleasant disposition that had preceded him. Moreover—perhaps on the advice of Tryon—he made several visits up to the Regulator country, and is said to have won their friendship and admiration by his kindly interest in them. Older North Carolina historians have claimed that most of the Regulators were Loyalists or Tories during the Revolution because of the influence of Martin. More recent research, though, has disproved this myth. Actually, out of the 883 known Regulators, 289 were Whigs or Patriots, 560 had no known Revolutionary status, and only 34 were known to be Tories.

Certainly Martin's office was not an enviable one. In addition to the usual subjects of contention between the King's representative in the province and the restless citizens, new and insurmountable problems loomed up on the horizon in the coming struggle between the mother country and the American colonies.

The first clash between Martin and his assembly came over the question of the sinking fund tax. This was a tax of one shilling per poll, levied in 1748, to pay for certain obligations, which the assemblymen of 1771 felt had already been met. Accordingly, the legislators rescinded the tax. The governor, however, held different views on the matter, and promptly vetoed the assembly's action, declaring it a fraud and a violation of public faith. In retaliation, the assembly drew up a resolution to idemnify or compensate the sheriffs for not collecting the tax. The governor thereupon played his trump card: he dissolved the assembly before the resolution could be entered in the journal. But he reckoned without Richard Caswell, Speaker of the House, who would be a leading Revolutionary patriot and the first governor of the independent state of North Carolina. Caswell immediately advised the treasurers that they could notify the sheriffs of each county (who were responsible for the collection of all taxes) that the taxes in question need not be collected. The governor made a last feeble effort by issuing a proclamation requiring the sheriffs to collect the revenues, but his orders were not carried out. The issue at stake remained a source of strife down to the Revolution.

Martin, who realized the assembly had won the upper hand, did not call a new one until January, 1773. With tensions between the mother country and the province becoming more taut, this assembly was in an even more independent, if not belligerent, mood. Almost immediately governor and assembly locked horns again, this time over the Tryon Court Law. This law, which, as usual, was enacted for only two years at a time, was about to expire and the maintenance and continuance of the whole judicial system was in jeopardy. The situation was complicated by the fact that the assembly proposed to tack onto the court law a provision giving the assembly the right to attach or seize the property in North Carolina of non-residents who owed debts in the province. This proposal was, of course, violently objected to by the

British merchants, and by Josiah Martin. The difference between the two opposing factions could not be solved. The governor, on instructions from England, stubbornly refused to approve any court bill which incorporated the attachment clause. The upshot was that after 1773 there were no courts in the province except those of the county magistrates, who could try only those civil cases involving less than £20, and only those criminal cases involving minor misdemeanors.

With the collapse of the court sytem, utter confusion reigned. In order to provide for the trial of criminal cases Governor Martin used the royal prerogative to create emergency criminal courts. But when the assembly met in December, 1773, they refused to bear the expenses of these bodies.

Increased dissatisfaction with British rule came as a result of the royal order in 1772 for running the North Carolina-South Carolina line farther west. In the resulting survey, North Carolina was deprived of land which many persons felt was rightfully hers.

One can easily understand and appreciate the mood of the assembly which met in New Bern on December 4, 1773. It will be remembered that the British Parliament had repealed the Stamp Act in 1766, but had accompanied the repeal with the Declaratory Act, which "declared" that Parliament had the right to tax the colonies in any way it saw fit. Accordingly, the next year it had slapped the Townshend Taxes upon the American provinces, by which a duty was laid upon paint, tea, paper, lead, and glass. But the reaction to these measures all up and down the Atlantic had been so violent that Parliament repealed these taxes too—all except the tax on tea. This levy was retained largely because of the lobbying efforts of the powerful East India Tea Company.

Then, in December, 1773, when ships laden with tea appeared in harbors along, the Atlantic Coast, "tea parties" greeted them. Contrary to popular American belief, Boston was not the only port which staged such parties, though no tea was dumped into any harbor except in Boston. But Newport, Philadelphia, New York, Baltimore, Norfolk, Charleston, Savannah, and Edenton, North Carolina, gave the tea shippers a merry time. In Edenton some fifty ladies signed a resolution refusing to buy or consume any English tea. This event, incidentally, marked the first organized political activity of a group of women anywhere in America.

The assembly was in session in New Bern in December, 1773, exactly at the same time the Boston Tea Party was taking place. With conditions as they were, they readily and eagerly accepted Virginia's recommendation that each colony appoint a Committee of Correspondence to keep in touch with the other colonies.

Meanwhile Britain reacted swiftly to the Boston Tea Party by closing the port of Boston and imposing other restrictions known as the Intolerable Acts. In North Carolina the majority of citizens felt that the cause of Boston was the cause of all the American colonies and the sloop *Penelope*, laden with corn, flour, and pork was immediately dispatched to the aid of the beleaguered northern city.

In June, 1774, the Massachusetts legislature issued a call for each colony to send delegates to a Continental Congress to meet in Philadelphia in September. In order to prevent North Carolina from sending a delegation, Governor Martin refused to summon the assembly. Whereupon, Colonel John Harvey, Speaker of the House, announced: "In that case the people will hold a convention independent of the Governor." This, of course, was a revolutionary statement, calling for an extra-legal, extra-constitutional convention. Only the

King, through his duly appointed governor, had that power, according to British law. Nevertheless, in complete defiance or British authority, a mass meeting was held in Wilmington in July at which Cornelius Harnett, William Hooper (who would be a signer of the Declaration of Independence), and others issued a call for a "provincial congress independent of the governor" to meet in New Bern on August 25.

Although the ensuing First Provincial Congress met for only three days, it is significant for the fact that it was clearly a revolutionary body. Among other accomplishments it chose William Hooper, Richard Caswell and Joseph Hewes as delegates to the Continental Congress. Henceforward the march of events toward the Revolution and the separation from the mother country was swift.

And it was manifestly impossible for Governor Martin to stem so strong a tide. Early in March of 1775 he was informed of the forming of troops in New Hanover and Brunswick counties. In April his council—composed of the richest and most influential men in the province—deserted him. In desperation he called the assembly to meet on April 4 in New Bern. But his authority was further defied when John Harvey issued a call for the Second Provincial Congress to meet at the same place the day before the regular assembly.

It is interesting to note that all but one of the fifty-two members of the assembly was also a member of the Provincial Congress, composed of sixty-seven members. Moreover, John Harvey served as both Speaker of the House and moderator of the latter body. With the revolutionary spirit having reached such a white heat, it is difficult to determine what Martin hoped to accomplish in calling the assembly. Maybe he felt he could impress them with the majesty of the King's representative, but this seems unlikely in the light of recent past events. Or maybe he called them together for the purpose of denouncing them. Certainly he did the latter in his address to them in which he urged that they resist "the monster, sedition, which has dared to raise his impious head in America." As for the extra-legal Provincial Congress he denounced it as "an insult" to the assembly and urged that it be repudiated.

The Provincial Congress on its part did not hesitate to denounce the governor and maintained its right to petition the King for redress of grievances. Among other achievements it reelected its delegates to the Continental Congress and authorized the creation of safety committees for each county and town, and for the province as a whole. The assembly endorsed virtually the same actions as the Congress and was angrily dissolved by the governor after a four-day session. Thus was brought to an end the last royal assembly in North Carolina.

In a spirt of sadness and resignation, Martin wrote the Earl of Dartmouth, Secretary of State for the Colonies, that his situation was "most despicable and mortifying" and that royal authority in the province was "as absolutely prostrate as impotent, and nothing but the shadow of it is left." He lamented that each day he saw

> indignantly the Sacred Majesty of my Royal Master insulted, the Rights of His Crown denied and violated, His Government set at naught, and trampled upon, his servants of highest dignity reviled, traduced, abused, the Rights of His Subjects destroyed by the most arbitrary usurpations, and the whole Constitution unhinged and prostrate, and I live alas ingloriously only to deplore it.

His conclusion was that unless effectual measures were taken there will not long remain a trace of Britain's dominions over these colonies.

Martin's predictions came true swiftly. On April 19 there occurred the battles of Lexington and Concord in Massachusetts. The Revolution had begun.

With the total collapse of royal government, safety committees took over to enforce the authority of the Provincial and Continental Congresses. These committees were denounced by Martin as being "motley mobs" and "promoters of sedition," and he issued a proclamation against them, but it fell on deaf ears.

But Martin had seen the handwriting on the wall as early as March, when he had sent an urgent letter to the British commander in Boston for arms and ammunition. Unknown to him, the letter was intercepted by the Whigs. As a protection he also planted the only cannon which he had—six of them—in front of the Palace, but these were carried off by what he called "a mob stimulated with liquor." He became so alarmed over the safety of his family that he sent them back to New York, and he himself, slipped out under cover of darkness, on the night of May 24, and fled to Fort Johnston on the Cape Fear below Brunswick. But even here he feared for his life and fled once more, this time to the safety of a British crusier, the *Cruzier,* lying off shore. Martin's fears were not groundless, because on July 18 a group of Whigs, led by Harnett, Ashe, and Robert Howe, burned Fort Johnston to the ground.

The assembly that was to convene in New Bern on July 12, 1775, was prorogued by Martin, who later decided not to call it at all. Royal authority had collapsed and there was little hope or chance of reviving it. Yet he could at least let go with a verbal salvo of denunciation. In a "Fiery Proclamation" on August 8 he directed his shots at the Revolutionary committees of safety which, he wrote, were guilty of circulating "the basest and most scandalous Seditions and inflammatory falsehoods," and that they were characterized by "evil, pernicious and traitorous Councils and influence." The reply of the Third Provincial Congress, which was called by Samuel Johnston, and which assembled August 20th in Hillsborough, was equally as scathing. It denounced the proclamation as "a false, scandalous, malacious and sedicious libel, tending to disunite the good people of this province, and to stir up tumults and insurrections, dangerous to the peace of His Majesty's Government, and the safety of the Inhabitants." It recommended that it be burned by the common hangman.

The Hillsborough convention prepared for war and also adopted the necessary financial measures to carry on the government and the war. But Martin, too, in his virtual prison on the *Cruzier* was preparing for war. As a matter of fact, he had worked out a most ambitious scheme for the reconquest of North Carolina and, indeed, of the entire South. In a lengthy letter to the Earl of Dartmouth, dated June, 30, 1775, Martin first humbly offered his own services in raising a battalion of a thousand Scottish Highlanders who had settled in the Cape Fear Valley, and who were largely Tories. He also requested to be restored to the rank of lieutenant colonel (which was flatly refused.) Secondly, General Thomas Gage was to supply arms and ammunition with which he could arm 3,000 Highlanders. Optimistically, Martin hoped that this nucleus would subsequently attract at least 20,000 of the estimated 30,000 fighting men in the province. This force, he wrote, would hold Virginia "in such awe" that no reinforcements would be sent to North Carolina, while the colonies to the south could be subjugated with little effort. Thirdly, Sir Peter Parker, in command of a British fleet of seventy-two sail, was to convoy seven regiments of British regulars, led by Lord Charles Cornwallis.

These were to effect a juncture at Wilmington about mid-February with 2,000 regulars from Boston, commanded by Sir Henry Clinton. Finally, they were to be joined by the Highlanders.

The scheme was eventually included in the basic plan for an expedition against Charleston. Martin, moreover, was instructed by Dartmouth to "loose no time in sending Emissaries amongst the Inhabitants of the well-disposed Counties with Authority and Commission to the principal persons of Trust and Confidence for raising and embodying as many men as can be procured."

As early as July, 1775, General Gage head sent Lieutenant Colonel Donald MacDonald and Captain Donald McLeod, two Highlanders officers, to North Carolina to recruit men for a battalion of the Royal Highland Emigrant Regiment. Martin worked untiringly with these men and others throughout the fall and winter. By mid-February the Highlanders came together first at Cross Hill (one mile west of present Carthage) and began their march down to Wilmington. A second rendezvous was held at Cross Creek (now Fayetteville) and the march continued, some 1,600 strong.

Little did they realize (communications were not then what they are now) that an opposing force of some 1,100 Whigs, directed by Colonel James Moore, but under the immediate leadership of Colonel Richard Caswell and Alexander Martin, was lying in wait for them. On the evening of February 26 the Whigs reached Moore's Creek, which flows into Black River about ten miles before the latter flows into the Cape Fear. There was a bridge over the creek and the Whigs knew the Highlanders would have to cross it. The Whigs, therefore, removed much of the flooring of the bridge and greased the round log sleepers with soft soap and tallow. The Highlanders, who reached the other side about daybreak the morning of the 27th, fell unsuspectingly into the trap. Suffice it to say that virtually the entire Tory army, bag and baggage, was captured or killed. If was, indeed, an overwhelming Whig victory and a crushing defeat for Martin's well-laid schemes.

To make matters worse, the powerful British forces did not arrive at the Cape Fear until May. Instead of finding a great host of Loyalists to meet them, they were greeted by a forlorn and dispirited governor.

Realizing that his cause was lost, at least for the time being, Martin joined the British fleet when it departed for Charleston. And North Carolina was without a royal governor—either in office or in hiding. But North Carolina had not seen the last of Josiah Martin. After a sojourn with his family at "Rockhall" on Long Island, in 1779, he joined the Clinton expedition against South Carolina. Later Martin accompanied Cornwallis in his two invasions of North Carolina. Both at Charlotte and at Hillsborough he issued flaming resolutions calling on the people to rally to the royal standard.

Lord Cornwallis wrote in 1787 in regard to Martin's services in the organization of Loyalists bands in North Carolina:

> I have constantly received the most zealous assistance from Governor Martin during my command in the southern district. Hoping that his presence would tend to excite the loyal subjects in this province to take an active part with us, he has cheerfully submitted to the fatigues of our campaign; but his delicate constitution has suffered by his public spirit, for, by the advice of the physicians, he is now obliged to return to England for the recovering of his health.

Martin, in fact, left Cornwallis at Wilmington in April, 1781, went to New York, presumably to pick up his family, and sailed for England. He died in London April 13, 1786. He had continued to draw his salary as governor until October, 1783, and was compensated for his North Carolina property which had been confiscated by the Whig government.

Professor A. Ray Newsome accurately sums up Josiah Martin's character and contribution as the last royal governor of North Carolina:

> Though a military man without previous political experience, somewhat stubborn and insistent on prerogative, and unappreciative of the colonial position, Martin was accomplished, energetic, able honest, faithful, as well as sincere and patient in his efforts to promote the public welfare and to conciliate the colony without violating his positive instructions and his conception of the duties of his office. He sought to become informed of conditions in the colony, to eliminate abuses in administration, and to pacify the Regulators, but he was not able to reconcile the tempers, aims, and political philosophies of colony and mother country.